3

WITHDRAWN

ONE WOMAN'S POWER

A BIOGRAPHY OF GLORIA STEINEM
by Sondra Henry & Emily Taitz
Afterword by Gloria Steinem

A People in Focus Book

P DILLON PRESS, INC.
Minneapolis, Minnesota 55415

Acknowledgments

We would like to thank Gloria Steinem for her gracious help and cooperation in granting us ample time for interviews, and searching her memory for details and dates to help us in our work. Our appreciation also goes to Susanne Steinem Patch, Letty Cottin Pogrebin, Florence Rapaport, founder of Womanspace in Great Neck, New York, and Sylvia Kramer of the Women's Action Alliance for sharing their knowledge and memories with us. Thank you also to Eleanor Lewis, archivist at the Smith College Archives, Northampton, Massachusetts, who aided us in our research, and to Doris Gold, publisher of Biblio Press, who has always been a source of encouragement.

Photographic Acknowledgments

Cover: Robert Deutsch, USA Today
Back and Flap: David Kaplan
Inside: from the collection of Gloria Steinem

Library of Congress Cataloging in Publication Data

Henry, Sondra.
   One woman's power.

   (People in focus)
   Bibliography: p.
   Includes index.
   Summary: A biography of the influential champion of women's rights with information on her childhood, her education, and her work in the women's movement.
     1. Steinem, Gloria—Juvenile literature. 2. Feminists—United States—Biography—Juvenile literature.
   [1. Steinem, Gloria. 2. Feminists] I. Taitz, Emily. II. Title. III. Series.
   HQ1413.S675H46 1987   305.4'2'0924 [B] [92]   86-11631
   ISBN 0-87518-346-8

Dillon Press, Inc., 242 Portland Avenue South
Minneapolis, Minnesota 55415

Printed in the United States of America
   2 3 4 5 6 7 8 9 10 96 95 94 93 92 91 90 89 88

/Contents

4

Introduction

You know how to make 'em listen

The Grand Ballroom of the Waldorf Astoria Hotel, in the heart of New York City, glittered and shone with seven hundred and fifty place settings of silver, china, and crystal. Celebrities from the worlds of politics, show business, publishing, and the women's movement had come together to make Gloria Steinem's fiftieth birthday one of the most spectacular events of 1984. An all-woman band played in her honor, and a chorus of famous women serenaded her with:

> "Glow little Gloria, glisten, glisten,
> You know how to make 'em listen. . ."

As Gloria looked out over a sea of faces, rows of tables decorated with pink and white peonies, and a thousand balloons, she could not help remembering that life had not always been so beautiful.

When she was young, her mother, an educated woman, suffered from a mental illness. This situation forced Gloria, before she was twelve, to take on many responsibilities, which made her childhood difficult and often unhappy. But in spite of it, Gloria never doubted her mother's love, and throughout those difficult years managed to hold on to her sense of self-worth. Years later, Gloria would view her mother's condition as the result of the loss of her work as a newspaper reporter and editor.

Her parents' divorce and her father's absence for long periods of time often forced Gloria and her mother to live on the edge of poverty. However, these experiences taught her how to cope with uncertainty, a lesson that proved useful in the early days of her career. In addition, the example of her father's life, unburdened by material possessions and unconcerned with security, would prove valuable, too.

As a teenager, Gloria Steinem dreamed of tap-dancing her way out of Toledo, Ohio, the town where she grew up. However, it was not her talent as a dancer, but her ability and hard work as a journalist that enabled her to transform her life. She became sensitive to women's issues partly through her own experiences and partly through her work as a journalist. At first a free-lance writer, she later became involved in the founding of *New York* magazine, and went on to become a co-founder and editor of *Ms.*, the first national feminist magazine in America since Susan B. Anthony edited

Revolution. Her personal commitment to women, as well as to poor and disadvantaged people all over the world, ultimately helped to make her famous.

Gloria Steinem has been in the forefront of some of the most significant events of recent times. As a leader in the women's movement, she manages to combine humor, a friendly style, and serious issues in a way that makes people sit up and listen. And the changes in her own life reflect events that have changed the lives and dreams of many girls and women.

Chapter/One

How can I take care of your mother?

Gloria's very first memory was of snuggling into Leo Steinem's large, comfortable lap to listen to a favorite radio program. Being with her father felt so much safer than being with her mother. Her mother was kind, of course, and sometimes hugged and kissed Gloria just like her father, but she often fussed and worried, too. At times Ruth Steinem was just there; she did not speak or smile, and remained in bed. She had done this for as long as Gloria could remember. Later, Gloria would come to understand that her mother was mentally ill and suffered from anxiety neurosis and agoraphobia (fear of being outside); but as a little girl, Gloria was told that her mother was just "that way."

She remembered driving around with her parents while her father looked for antiques to buy and resell. With her older sister Sue off at school, and Gloria too young to stay alone, she was often brought along on these day trips. Sometimes she was allowed to help her father carry paper-wrapped bundles out to the car where her mother, sitting silently, was waiting for them. They packed their treasures into the back seat, and on they drove to the next stop.

Those were fine, safe memories. Holding her father's hand made her happy, and remembering how his strong arms lifted her up and swung her around made her feel good.

Because Gloria did not go to school regularly, she had few memories of school friends or teachers. Instead, she remembered winters traveling with her parents and Sue in a dome-topped trailer packed tight with their belongings. They would head south to Florida or west to California, where the weather was warmer. Wherever they went, her father continued trying to make a living by finding and selling antiques.

But Gloria's best memories were of the summers. At Clark Lake, Michigan, wearing a red bathing suit, she roamed around the small colony of resort bungalows on the edge of the lake. Sometimes she slept in the office of Ocean Beach Pier, an entertainment hall that her father owned and managed. There he planned shows and hired bands to perform for vacationing families. Gloria loved to talk with the people who worked there and listen to the bands practicing for the evening's show. It was here that she first dreamed of being a performer. In fact, when she had been born, on March 25, 1934, Ruth and Leo Steinem announced her birth with a card that read "Gloria Marie Steinem—8-1/2 Pound Blues Singer—World Premier Appearance." At Ocean Beach Pier, Ruby Brown, the cigarette girl, taught Gloria her first tap dance steps. The little girl danced to the music of Joe Venuti, a jazz violinist, and learned chords on the piano from the pianists in many bands. How long ago those days would seem to Gloria when she was ten.

The memories of the times after her father's Ocean Beach Pier closed were sometimes good ones, too. She remembered going to the movies with her father, and sipping malteds with him at the drugstore counter. He had made her feel so grown up at those times.

Her most vivid memory, though, was when the family broke up. Her sister Sue went back to college, and Leo, who had already closed the business at Clark Lake, went off to California as he always did after the summer. But this time, Ruth and Gloria left, too. They went to Amherst, Massachusetts, to live near Sue's college for one year.

In Amherst, Gloria attended the fifth grade. But things did not work out. A year later, they returned to Toledo, Ohio, the place where Gloria's parents had been born, and where they had met and married.

Gloria remembered that her father had once asked, "How can I travel and take care of your mother, too?"

She knew her father had to travel to make a living, and though she was very young, she understood that they needed the money for food and clothes, for her

mother's medicine and Sue's college education. Gloria
also knew she wanted to be a dancer, and longed for
dancing lessons, too.

Although she wished they could travel with her
mother and father in the trailer like they had done
before, Gloria realized that she had to stay in one place
and go to school. But that was not the only problem. As
young as she was, Gloria understood that Leo Steinem
had reached the end of his rope. He had tried to keep
the family together, but he was a restless man who
could not settle down for long.

"I want to be a dancer," Gloria told him firmly, and
her father promised that she would get dancing lessons
and maybe even piano lessons, too, with the extra
money he would earn. And so, he left.

When Leo Steinem went on the road, Gloria remained alone with her mother. Somehow, Gloria understood he had to go, and did not resent it. Even as an
adult, when she talks about her father's decision to
leave, she is not angry. She knew he was doing the best
he could.

She and her mother settled into a small apartment in
Toledo, and Gloria began the sixth grade. A year later,
when she was beginning junior high school, they moved
to 747 Woodville Road, the house where her mother
had grown up. It was an old house, often cold and
drafty, with a sagging front porch and only a few pieces
of furniture. There was one big bed, which Gloria
shared with her mother to keep warm.

At eleven or twelve, it was not easy for Gloria to take care of her mother, go to school, and still find time for her friends and the tap dancing lessons she loved. Often Gloria longed for a home like other children, with a mother who would cook, clean, help her with homework, and care for her when she was sick.

Once, she had been told, her mother had been different. She had gone to college at Oberlin University and the University of Toledo where she had met Leo Steinem. Before and after Sue was born, Ruth had worked as a reporter for the Toledo *Blade*. She had first become mentally ill—it was called a "nervous breakdown" then—before Gloria was born, when Sue was five years old. Only after months in a sanatorium (a rest home) did she recover enough to come home and work with Leo Steinem at the Michigan resort. However, she was not completely without spells of depression and anxiety, and after Gloria was born, Ruth regularly took a tranquilizing medicine to keep from being fearful.

Sometimes Gloria hated her mother's medicine, because it made Ruth's speech slurred and made other people—neighbors and school friends—think she was drunk. Gloria had to fix their meals, shop for food, and try to keep the house in order.

At other times, though, it seemed to her that if Ruth didn't take the medicine, she would not be able to sleep at all, and her anxiety would shatter her completely. Gloria especially remembered one awful Thanksgiving weekend, when she was in the eighth grade. Ruth had stopped taking the medicine, been sleepless for days, and imagined that they were being attacked by German soldiers. In a frantic effort to help her family escape, she plunged her hand through the window. Gloria, hearing the screams and running in, saw her mother with blood running down her arm from where the glass had cut her. Gloria tried to calm and reassure her. Nothing helped. Then she remembered the medicine. Before her mother agreed to take it, Gloria sat with her that whole day, gripping her bandaged hand, fearing that she might hurt herself again. She hung onto Ruth with one hand, her assignment for school in the other, until at last, her mother took the medicine. Gloria finally calmed her own fears and lost herself completely in her book for a few hours.

It was on days like those that Gloria realized her mother needed "Dr. Howard's medicine" as a relief from the terrible fears that haunted her, and so that Gloria could have some time to be a teenager.

When her mother was at her worst, Gloria, too, dreamed. "She is not really my mother," Gloria told herself. She imagined that she was adopted. One day, she thought, her real parents would come and claim her, and life would be wonderful. Meanwhile, she escaped by seeing Saturday matinee movies with her friends, just as years earlier she had escaped by dreaming she was Shirley Temple, the little girl movie star from Hollywood.

Gloria also read all kinds of books—mysteries, novels, philosophy, and books about horses and dancing—whenever she could squeeze in the extra time. Her favorite author was Louisa May Alcott, whom Gloria considered to be her friend. She often imagined that this great writer had come back to life and Gloria was showing her around the world. She spent many pleasant hours dreaming of what she would show her.

Occasionally, there was no money for movies. Leo Steinem had gone to California to make a living, but he often had no money to send to his family. Sometimes, the only income Gloria and her mother had was the rent from the downstairs apartment of their house, which barely paid for their necessities. Gloria got school clothes once a year when Aunt Jeanette Brand, her mother's sister, took her shopping. Aunt Janey, as she was called, also paid for some of Sue's clothes.

Still, Gloria managed the Saturday movies most of the time, and dancing lessons, too. Gloria loved to dance. As she tapped and whirled, all her worries seemed to drop away. She was a good dancer and sometimes taught classes to pay for her own lessons, or earned ten dollars for her performances at the Toledo Eagles Club or at local school shows.

On the rare days when Ruth felt better, Gloria could catch a glimpse of the capable, adventurous woman that other people had known. During those times, Gloria tried to share with her mother her dreams of show business and dancing. Once, Ruth took her for an audition with an amateur acting troupe that performed

Biblical dramas. She got a small part in *Noah's Ark*, and Ruth remained well long enough to help the group backstage with props and sound effects.

In more cheerful moments, Gloria told herself that life was not so sad. In addition to doing well in school, she had grown up to be pretty enough to have won second place in a Toledo beauty contest. She was tall and slim, with sparkling brown eyes and shiny dark hair that fell to her shoulders with a slight wave. Her pleasant manner and sense of humor won her many friends. She had steady boyfriends, too. She wore Joe's school ring on a chain around her neck for many months, and loyally attended football games while he was on the team. Later in her high school career, Ron replaced him as her "steady."

When Ruth was well she was up and around, trying to clean up the littered living room or planting flowers in the empty lot next door. Gloria and Ruth might visit Grandmother Marie Nuneviller, who was now old and ill most of the time. Sometimes Uncle Ed Steinem, Leo's brother, came to see them. Uncle Ed was good at repairing things. He helped keep their run-down oil burner going during the winter.

From her mother, Gloria learned about her father and the rest of her family. Ruth and Leo's marriage had displeased both their parents because Leo Steinem was Jewish and Ruth Nuneviller was Protestant.

Gloria's mother had also explained Gloria's Jewish heritage from her father's side, and told Gloria about the terrible things the Germans had done to the Jews in Europe during World War II. From those conversations, Gloria saw some of the sources of Ruth's fears for her and her sister, and understood that her mother's imagined terrors had been real for some families.

Despite her part-time jobs, money was always a serious problem, and caring for her mother was becoming more difficult, too. Through it all, Gloria continued studying, dancing, working, and going out with friends.

During Gloria's junior year at school, Ruth once again sank into a depression. Gloria did not know what to do. Medical help did not seem possible. Memories of a visit to her mother's doctor, back when she had been in the seventh grade, had never left her.

"Yes," the doctor had said, after speaking with Ruth, "she should definitely be in a state hospital." But Gloria could not agree. Even then, barely in her teens, she had read awful stories in local papers and *Life* magazine about the neglect of patients in state hospitals. The possibility of her mother getting better in a hospital had somehow seemed unlikely. In the 1930s and 1940s, mental health problems were even less understood than they are now. The family tended to blame Ruth for her own behavior, to believe that she could change if she really wanted to, or simply to think that she could not change and had to be cared for.

It was not until Gloria was older that doctors began to understand mental illness better, and to treat it like other diseases. But before that understanding was

there, Gloria felt that she should not condemn her
mother to a hopeless life in a hospital. She had taken
Ruth home from the doctor. She never regretted her
decision, even when her mother was at her worst and
didn't leave the bedroom for days at a time. Now,
however, things were more complicated.

In addition to Ruth's illness, daily living was becoming more difficult. The old house they occupied was
in complete disrepair, and rats from the abandoned
garage in back sometimes ran through the rooms at
night. They could no longer rent the downstairs apartment. In spite of Uncle Ed's best efforts, the Toledo
Health Department had condemned their old furnace
and sealed it up tightly.

Gloria did not know how they could manage another year, her last year of high school, with all these
problems. Her father and mother were now divorced,
and Sue was living in Washington. Now Gloria, too,
wanted to plan for her future, but no one offered practical help. Her mother, lying helpless in bed or sitting in
the shabby living room where Gloria had once shaped
piles of newspapers into makeshift chairs, somehow
realized her disappointment.

"I'm sorry, I'm sorry," Ruth would say with resigna-
tion whenever Gloria attempted to talk to her. But
Gloria was not ready to be resigned to whatever life
might offer her. She was close to despair as she thought
of the problems of a heatless house, lack of money, and
the burden of a sick mother. Complaining was useless,

Chapter/Two

These truly have been special years

When Gloria moved in with Sue and Sue's friends in a Washington, D.C. house, she enrolled at Western High School for her senior year. She worked hard at her studies. Being elected Vice President of her class and chosen as a princess-in-waiting at Western High School's Regimental Ball were exciting events. But most thrilling was the letter she received from Smith College in Northampton, Massachusetts.

Gloria knew about Smith College for Women because her sister Sue had gone there and graduated in 1946. Smith was one of the best women's colleges in the East, and Gloria had hoped her high school grades would be good enough for her to be accepted there. Although her grades had not been as high as she wanted, a friendly high school counselor had seen her potential ability, recommended strongly to Smith that she be accepted—and she was.

The green lawns and dignified colonial buildings of Smith College impressed Gloria immediately. As she and Sue entered the campus, carrying an assortment of old suitcases, boxes, and bundles, she felt that it must be the most beautiful place in the world. The freshly painted white columns against the red brick were echoed by a clump of white birch trees, bright against the still-green grass of early fall. Paradise Pond, tucked into a small ravine and circled with inviting paths and benches set under the trees, enchanted her the moment she caught sight of it. Gloria would spend the next four years at this school, and perhaps felt, even at first glance, that this beautiful place would transform her life forever.

In Toledo, most of Gloria's high school friends had not even considered college. In the 1950s, girls usually expected to get married as soon as they finished high school. But Gloria's parents and sister had been to college and wanted her to be well-educated as well. Even when Gloria herself dreamed only of dancing with the Rockettes on the grand stage at Radio City Music Hall in New York City, she expected to have a college education.

The money from the sale of the old house in Toledo, together with financial aid from Smith, made it possible for Gloria to begin college. Even the burden of caring for her mother had been lifted. After Ruth's year with Leo was over, Sue had made arrangements for Ruth to come to Washington and live with her. Later, in Gloria's second year at Smith, Ruth would at last go to a hospital to get the treatment she needed.

Entering Smith in September of 1952, Gloria breathed in the fresh New England air, and looked forward to meeting her fellow students. Sue helped her settle into her dorm. Afterwards, Gloria signed up for classes and read the freshman handbook in preparation for a test on the rules and regulations of the school.

Gloria soon learned that she was different from many of the other girls, not only in her interest in learning, but in her entire background. Many years later, after she had finished college and become a reporter, Gloria was to advise others: "Don't worry about your background; whether it's odd or ordinary, use it, build on it." That advice seems simple, but for Gloria it was a realization that came gradually, through learning to live with many girls from a variety of backgrounds.

Gloria found that each of them had something very different but equally important to offer to others. When Gloria discovered that her French was weak, one friend, Nancy Howard, who had been taught privately by a French tutor, helped her with grammar and translations. In return, Gloria helped Nancy put on makeup, a skill she had learned during her dancing experience in Toledo. Nancy, raised in a home with servants, was delighted when Gloria taught her to iron, and repaid her by pressing all Gloria's dresses along with her own. Who would have thought that knowing how to iron would be important in college?

Gloria got a much smaller monthly allowance from home than many girls did. She was proud of her independence and found that many of her new friends envied her for it. Although they might laugh at her midwestern-style blue jeans, hopelessly out of fashion, it was good-natured fun. They respected Gloria for her helpfulness, her even temper, and her ability.

College classes and activities such as working at a nearby mental hospital, or waiting tables at dinners for guest speakers filled Gloria's days, but by far the best thing about being at Smith was the books. When one of her classmates complained, and another dropped out and went home, Gloria was amazed. As she said later, thinking back on her college years: "Any place which served three meals a day and gave me as many books as I wanted to read was pure heaven."

Although in her sophomore year she did dance in musical shows at Smith and also at nearby Amherst College, dancing never again was her first love. Gloria was pursuing a major in government, and politics and political ideas were what interested her the most. She had learned a little about government during her year in Washington, D.C. and as a volunteer for Adlai Stevenson, that year's Democratic candidate for president. She had helped write and print up a student newsletter about Stevenson the summer after her high school graduation. Her work for him would be the first of many political commitments that Gloria would make throughout her life.

At Smith, the presidential campaign was in full swing. Each week Smith's paper, *The Sophian*, featured an article about the upcoming elections. One week an article would discuss General Dwight D. Eisenhower, the Republican candidate, and the next week would focus on Stevenson. Gloria read them with interest. She discovered, to her surprise, that most of her classmates preferred "Ike" (as everyone called the General), while her professors favored her own candidate, Stevenson. On election night, listening to the radio well past the 10:15 P.M. curfew to find out the results, it seemed that the students had been better predictors than their teachers: Eisenhower was the new president.

With the election over, political disagreement among the young women was quickly put aside, and Gloria went back to her studies. Very soon, everyone's thoughts were on holiday parties, and talk at the dinner table in the college dorm centered around what they wanted for Christmas. Camel hair coats, bathing suits for trips to the Bahamas, and family vacation plans were all discussed. Gloria could not help but compare her friends' lives to her own and to think about the differences. She knew that Sue was in Washington awaiting her return. There would be gifts from her father and her aunts and uncles in Toledo. However, the festive celebrations her classmates anticipated would not be part of her holiday.

That Christmas it was nice to come home, help Sue trim the Christmas tree, and visit old friends from high school. But her mother's condition troubled Gloria. She seemed more depressed and frightened than ever, and Sue was arranging for her to go to a special hospital and receive treatment. Gloria kissed Ruth and gave her the presents she had brought, but Ruth seemed to be in a world of her own.

After Gloria returned to college, she still worried about her mother, and thought about the discussions she'd had with Sue concerning hospital care and treatment. She did not talk about family problems to her friends at Smith, and never thought she had the right to be grouchy or unhappy because of them. But her ideas about showing her feelings changed during her college days. Gloria was able to pinpoint that particular lesson exactly. One morning at breakfast a friend sat opposite her, sipping coffee and looking grumpy.

"What's the matter?" Gloria asked.

"Nothing is the matter," came the answer. "I'm just in a bad mood."

Gloria was amazed. How could anyone be "in a bad mood" for no reason? If you were really sick, or had been in an accident, or had lost all your money—those were real reasons for unhappiness. But to be sad for no particular reason, and to have it accepted by other people, was a new idea for Gloria. She began to realize that it was all right to feel sad for nothing, to be in a bad mood, even to have fights with friends. This realization was important because it gave Gloria the security she needed to be herself and accept her feelings.

Semesters passed quickly at Smith. The teachers liked Gloria's writing and made encouraging comments about her talents. She knew that her previous school record had not been the best, but she soon discovered that her abilities and her own unique experiences more than made up for the private schools and language tutors her friends had enjoyed. Gloria, the girl who had never attended any school for a complete year until the sixth grade, was a "Smithie" who found time to rehearse for Rally Day performances, help decorate for Carnival, and cram before an important exam. By the end of sophomore year, she had become part of Smith College in every way and loved the opportunity it offered her for learning.

Success in school brought with it the chance to study abroad. During her third year, Gloria traveled to Geneva, Switzerland, where Smith ran its own program along with the University of Geneva. Many of the government majors chose to study there, and since the courses were given in French, Gloria had an opportunity to use the language she had worked so hard to learn. She would also be able to travel.

The year in Europe fulfilled all of Gloria's expectations. Life in Geneva was very different than it had been in the little New England town of Northampton. Not only were the language and the country different, but every day the women students wore suits and dresses and high heeled shoes to classes instead of Bermuda shorts or blue jeans. The women took turns living in a hotel or with Swiss families near the University, so there was always a new experience on the horizon.

When the year was over, Gloria, ready and even eager to return home, felt like a world traveler, prepared for anything. But first, there was one more year—her last—at Smith. Senior Gloria Steinem was a successful student. For her outstanding grades she had achieved membership in Phi Beta Kappa, the international honor society whose members all had the highest grades at college. She was also a candidate for honors in her major, government, and was elected senior class historian. It was as historian that she had the opportunity to write about her feelings that spring of 1956, in the Smith *Alumnae Quarterly*. She recalled all the exciting activities of her years at Smith: the lectures, the chance to hear great scholars and discuss important issues, as well as the shows presented on Rally Day, the impressive college ceremonies, and the sporting events. "Looking at things for the last time," wrote Gloria, "makes colors brighter and detail more clear." In that article she gave a new name to her feelings about leaving Smith College for good. She called it "the senior disease, Lastimeitis."

In spite of the sadness at leaving, Gloria was ready to look ahead. The most exciting prospect for the near future was her scholarship to study in India. Chester Bowles, the Ambassador to India under President Eisenhower, had come to speak at Smith, and with his speaker's fee had established the Chester Bowles Asian

Fellowship. Vera Micheles Dean, a professor at Smith with whom Gloria had taken a course on India, recommended that she apply for the scholarship. It offered the chance to explore another part of the world, as well as the chance to get away from a commitment at home.

During her senior year, Gloria, like many of her classmates, had accepted an engagement ring from her newest boyfriend, Blair. She had met him through her friend Nancy Howard, who had left Smith a few years before to be married. Although Gloria had thought she loved Blair, and had pictured a life with him at one time, she had since been filled with doubts. Was an engagement really what she wanted? She had become engaged and then changed her mind. But Blair had persuaded her to try again. He was a newspaper columnist. Although the interesting life he led was attractive to Gloria, being with him was not as important to her as time to develop herself, to find out what she could do on her own. Just now she didn't really want to marry Blair or anyone else.

The fellowship came through for her, and even though it was only a thousand dollars, hardly enough for her to live on, she was eager to accept. Years before, her father had taught her how to live with insecurity, so she was not afraid of it. She decided to find a way to tell Blair that they could not get married. Now, she felt, she could go to India and study.

The day of graduation, Saturday, June 3, 1956, Gloria marched down the aisle. As she took her seat she caught a glimpse of her sister Sue, married now and with a child at home in Washington, D.C. Seated beside Sue was Ruth, out of the hospital now, and Leo, here from the West for this special event. They were all smiling proudly.

Gloria adjusted the square cap on her head, sat up straight in her chair, and listened to poet Archibald MacLeish, the speaker at her class graduation. "These truly have been special years," she thought. Gloria felt that Smith had been the best of all possible schools. She had loved being there. Now she was leaving, and eager for new experiences.

Chapter/Three

Too much of everything

"I didn't know how not to get married," Gloria would say years later, "so I went to India." But it was more than a desire to run away that brought her there. She had sympathized with poor and oppressed people, with whom she had identified, ever since childhood. The influence of her classes in government at Smith, and even her work on Adlai Stevenson's presidential campaign, had helped her decide that she wanted to make a real contribution to the world.

In 1957 India was a struggling country which had gained its independence from England just ten years before. Indians were working hard to develop modern technology, help their people out of poverty, and remain democratic. Gloria felt that if she wanted to help people, this was a good place to begin.

On the long flight from London, England, to Bombay, India, Gloria had had time to think about the events of the last few months, beginning with her broken engagement. Because she feared that she would give in and marry Blair if she stayed in America, she went to England to wait for her visa to India. A college friend, Jane Bird, now married to an Englishman, had offered her a bed in her own house, and Gloria had found work as a waitress in an espresso café. That way, she could save money for her journey and put Blair behind her.

Gloria gradually realized that she had a serious problem. At first she didn't want to believe that her missed periods meant that she was pregnant, but a doctor confirmed that she was.

With the news came feelings of great despair. At that time, being unmarried and having a child was a terrible disgrace and was disapproved of by almost everyone. Children without fathers were often outcasts and suffered as much as their mothers. For Gloria, there seemed to be nothing to do but return to New York and marry Blair—a decision that Gloria had already determined was wrong for her. She felt strongly that she had to find out who she was and what she could accomplish before she gave birth to someone else. Gloria was so desperate that she even thought about ending her life. Then, a chance meeting alerted her to another option.

In 1956, in England as in the United States, abortion was against the law. But at a party, Gloria met an American playwright who was producing a show in

England. He was speaking about arranging abortions for two actresses in the cast. With a casualness and unconcern she did not feel, Gloria remarked, "I thought abortions were illegal in England."

The American explained that although they were, it was not difficult to get two doctors to sign a paper saying that it would be bad for your health—mental or physical—to have a child. Then, abortion was legal.

The next day Gloria went back to the doctor and confided her problem to him. She told him of her boyfriend back in New York, her plans to go to India, and her fear of having an unwanted child that she could not care for. The doctor listened without a word. Then he picked up a pen, wrote down the name of another doctor, and handed her the sheet of paper she needed.

"You must promise me two things," said the doctor to Gloria. "First, that you will never tell anyone what I have done, and second, that you will go to India and finish what you have set out to do."

Gloria kept silent for years. The day of the abortion, no one knew where she had gone, not even her friend Jane. She had been frightened and alone. But when it was over, a feeling of relief washed over her as she realized she would not be forced to have the unwanted baby that she was unable to care for.

The memory of those feelings of fear and despair would come back to Gloria years later. Because of her own experience, which had been buried inside her for so many years, Gloria was able to understand how other

women felt about unwanted pregnancies. Before the
1970s, abortions were not legally available in the United
States. She helped organize women's fight to control
their own bodies and to determine for themselves when
an abortion was essential.

Now, stepping down from the TWA plane into the
hot night air of Bombay, India, Gloria was ready for
anything. By midnight, she had passed through customs and been sprayed with insect spray, in case any
insect pests were traveling on her body. She wanted to
stay in a nearby youth hostel, but discovered that it was
full. A helpful TWA employee, Jim Farley, saw her
plight and invited her home to meet his wife and family.

Riding along in Farley's car, Gloria saw rows of
people sleeping on the streets on wooden frame beds
called *charpoys*. Still others were without beds and
simply curled up in doorways, wrapped in rags. This
first sight of what Gloria later labeled "Asian poverty"
would remain with her all her life. It made her even
more uncomfortable as Mrs. Farley, her gracious host-
ess, showed her their lovely apartment with marble
floors, located in a prosperous part of Bombay.

The next day, outside in the streets, Gloria could see
what seemed like thousands of people walking with
bundles on their backs, driving in wagons, riding bicy-
cles, or packed tightly into buses. The streets were
crowded with men and women of many types and
colors. She recalled a quote about India that she had
read before her trip: "Too many people, too many

animals, too many customs, too many gods—too much of everything!"

After a few days at the Farleys, Gloria left for New Delhi, where she met Kayla Achter, another scholarship student from Smith. They registered for classes at Delhi University and decided to live at Miranda House, a dormitory and a women's college. Gloria and Kayla crossed the dusty, red-clay paths of the campus, which had long, barracks-like cement block buildings. The red brick and green grass of Smith College seemed very far away—and indeed it was. Nevertheless, after the two hundred women residents of Miranda House welcomed Gloria and Kayla with kindness and curiosity, their homesickness soon disappeared. They were the first American students to live in the dorms of Miranda House.

Gloria was happy to get to know many Indian people as individuals. Her classmates invited her to their homes, and she learned about their customs and daily lives. Soon she felt more at home in India than she ever had in Europe.

Exploring New Delhi, Gloria would cross the Jumna River and enter the old city, where she could wander the narrow streets. Here, she would pass men in *dhotis*, the traditional dress of Hindu working men, and women in brightly colored saris carrying stacks of brass water pails on their heads. She would peer into little booths where astrologers told people their fortunes according to the stars; wander through the market; and

breathe in the aromatic smells of spices, fresh vege-
tables, and cow dung. (Cows wandered freely in the
streets because they were sacred to people of the
Hindu faith.)

At the university, Kayla and Gloria were drawn into
discussions both in class and out. For the first time, they
heard American history from a Marxist (communist)
point of view, and often found themselves trying to
explain American foreign policy. In their rooms at
Miranda House, they stayed up late into the night
discussing such topics as the Christian idea of God and
the good and bad points of communism and democracy, as well as the American dating system and west-
ern-style lingerie! For fun, they were often asked to sing
American songs or dance for their Indian friends, who
returned the favor with songs and dances of India.

The winter months were the wedding season in India, and Gloria was invited to many celebrations. She
enjoyed seeing the beautiful clothes of the wedding
party—the groom, dressed like a prince, with jasmine
flowers hanging down from his turban, and the bride
in a red and gold sari.

Gloria learned to put on a sari, and was encouraged
by her Indian classmates to wear one daily. A sari con-
sists of a flat, long piece of fabric which is wound
around the waist to make a long skirt with pleats on
one side and then draped over one shoulder. In one of
her reports to Smith College, she wrote, "Saris make
one stand straighter, walk more slowly, and worry less

about time and efficiency." Her Indian friends seemed pleased when they saw that Gloria had adopted the Indian woman's traditional dress.

Gloria's interest in helping people had deepened during her stay in India, and she became involved in the problems of this struggling country. She learned that most Indians lived in small villages, under poorer conditions than anyone she had ever met in her life. Some land distribution had taken place. Yet a few rich people still owned most of the land while the vast majority of the Indian people had to pay rent to farm the land and owned nothing—neither property nor money. These tenant farmers were no longer content to accept their poverty as they once had. There were many complaints to the government and even riots in villages all over India.

Gloria was not the only one who saw how unfair the old landlord-tenant system was. Many Indian people were working to correct the problem. One of them was a man named Vinoba Bhave, leader of the *Bhoodan*, or land gift movement. At a meeting to discuss redistributing land, Gloria heard of Bhave's plan to walk through India with a group of followers and to try and convince landlords to give up part of their land to those who had none. Gloria was encouraged to join this walk by other Indian land reformers who felt that the presence of a woman would encourage other women to join them.

The idea of walking through India to unite the people and to protest government policy was first devel-

oped by Mahatma Gandhi, the great leader who helped
the Indians achieve independence from England. Following the tradition of the *sadhus*, India's holy men,
the walkers took nothing with them but a begging bowl
and the clothing that they wore, in order to show their
trust in God. Gloria did the same, adding only a comb
to keep her long hair neat and manageable.

For many weeks, Gloria followed Vinoba Bhave as
he walked calmly among the crowds. He pleaded, explained, and arranged compromises in order to encourage landlords to turn some of their land over to the
landless. From that walk, Gloria learned what idealism
and determination could accomplish. She would remember this technique years later, when she helped
organize political events in America to advance the
women's movement.

"I was never afraid," Gloria said afterwards about
her walk through India and her encounters with rioting
peasants. She explained that staying with other women
was the safest thing to do. Women were less aggressive
and would rarely be involved in violence. This, too, was
a lesson which she was to use again in America.

Before Gloria left India, she agreed to write a guide
book for the Indian government. The purpose was to
encourage more American students and professors to
travel and study in India, and to show the traveler the
images and faces of the land that Gloria had come to
love. She named her book *A Thousand Indias*.

Ruth Steinem, Gloria's mother, as a young woman.

(Top) *Gloria at Ocean Beach Pier, her father's resort in Michigan. Gloria was born there and the family lived at the resort until 1945.*
(Bottom) *Gloria (right) and her older sister, Susanne, at Ocean Beach Pier.*

Gloria on her way to the library. She loved to read and made regular trips to the library wherever she lived.

(Top) *Gloria (center) with two friends in Toledo.*
(Bottom) *Gloria's family at Susanne's graduation from Smith College in 1946.*
(Left to right) Aunt Janey, Ruth Steinem, Gloria, Sue, and Grandmother Marie
Nuneviller.
(Opposite page) *A high school portrait of Gloria.*

(Top) *Gloria performing in Toledo. She often earned money as a dancer during high school.*
(Bottom) *Gloria (center) in Paris. She spent 1955, her junior year of college, studying in Geneva, Switzerland, which gave her the opportunity to travel throughout Europe.*

Gloria wearing a sari, the traditional dress of Indian women. In 1957 she studied and worked in India, where she became involved in that country's land gift movement.

Gloria as she appeared in the February 1964 issue of Glamour. *She wrote for this magazine, which occasionally used its women writers as models.*

Chapter/Four

Between a career and marriage

Gloria's year in India went by very quickly. She returned to the United States convinced that she had to tell the world what she now understood about the poverty and problems of the East. "I must have been a terrible pain," she recalled, thinking back on those days. Gloria had become more conscious of politics than ever before, and of how the United States and the Soviet Union were both trying to win the loyalty of nations like India. Once back in New York, she wanted to be a writer and share with others all she had learned.

It was exciting to return home. Her mother was better after years of treatment, and it was wonderful to see her father and Sue and to visit with Sue's growing family. To them, and to everyone who knew her, Gloria had somehow become a celebrity. She was invited to speak at Smith College about her experiences in India, and was photographed for the school newspaper.

While visiting relatives in Toledo, she was interviewed by the Toledo *Blade,* and told the reporter all about her trip. She admitted to finally visiting that most famous of Indian sights, the Taj Mahal, even though she had not planned to. "I was determined to be the only living person never to visit it," Gloria laughingly said to the reporter.

After the excitement of homecoming, however, disappointment quickly set in. Despite Gloria's enthusiasm and energy, she could not find work as a writer. In 1958 most publishers did not employ women to write about politics, and New Yorkers were not as interested in her experiences in India as her family and friends had been. She badly needed a job.

Finally, through a friend she had first met in India, an opportunity arose to work for an association called Independent Service for Information. The group, based in Cambridge, Massachusetts, was working to encourage American students to go to Communist Youth festivals and talk about democracy. Someone was needed to run the two-person office, speak to students at colleges, and write educational material. At the time, it seemed like a chance to work for democracy, and Gloria was soon involved with her new project.

Visiting colleges, meeting American students, and even going to a youth festival in Vienna were all part of her work. Through the Independent Service for Information, she encouraged students to go abroad armed with the sort of information about the diversity of

America and its politics and government that she herself would have liked in India.

When she began working, Gloria was very idealistic. She believed that discussion about the benefits and disadvantages of communism and democracy was very important. Years later, in 1967, Gloria learned that the Central Intelligence Agency (CIA) had secretly been funding the organization. Gloria was accused of working for the CIA and not for the students who attended these meetings. "I learned," she later said of her involvement with the CIA, "not to do anything that cannot be written about in newspapers."

In 1960 she returned to New York and again began to look for a job in publishing. After days of talking with friends and going to interviews, she landed a job with a new, small satire magazine called *Help! For Tired Minds*. The editor, Harvey Kurtzman, had been one of the originators of the well-known humor magazine, *Mad*. Now he was starting his own publication and needed an assistant.

Gloria worked for him first at home and then in the magazine's tiny office. Part of her job was to contact famous Hollywood and TV stars and ask them to appear on the cover of *Help!* magazine. To her boss's amazement, they almost always agreed. But Gloria herself was not surprised. Her years spent traveling and meeting people had taught her to expect a friendly response, even from strangers. She liked people, and with her charming smile, she could pursuade them to do almost anything. Her friends still repeated the story of how Gloria had somehow convinced executives of Pan American Airlines to give her a free ticket to India when she had no money to buy one.

Gloria's soft-spoken friendliness, combined with a keen mind and good manners, made her a woman people liked to be with. Harvey Kurtzman liked her, too. He introduced all of his friends to his capable and charming assistant, and she soon was invited to parties where she began to meet famous men and women in the publishing world, as well as in the arts and politics.

One of the most prominent people she met was John Kenneth Galbraith, a famous economist from Harvard University. She met him through his wife, Catherine (Kitty), a Smith College graduate whom she had gotten to know while working in Cambridge. Galbraith had just been appointed ambassador to India, so Gloria's familiarity with that country provided them with much to talk about. Gloria admired him for his experience and knowledge. From listening to his ideas, she learned much about economics—how things are produced and distributed in society.

Bob Benton was another of Gloria's new friends. He was the art director of *Esquire*, a popular men's magazine. Through him, she met many of the magazine's writers and editors, visited their offices, and saw how an editorial staff operated. Eventually, she started suggesting ideas for articles, and *Esquire* began to accept them.

Gloria's friendship with Bob Benton grew into love,

and they talked of marriage and a future together. They also worked together and encouraged each other in their careers. In addition to her work at *Help!*, Gloria had been contributing ideas and articles to several other magazines. She had also sold the outline for a special college issue to the editors of *Esquire.* Her career was advancing and her personal life was happy.

In September of 1962, Gloria's first big break came. There in the glossy pages of *Esquire* was her first by-line, the first time her name had appeared with something she had written in a national magazine. The article was part of the *Esquire* college issue, and although most of the readers were men, Gloria had written on a serious topic from a woman's point of view. She discussed the problems faced by young women, both in and out of college, who had to make decisions about sex in a world where attitudes regarding the roles of men and women were changing. The article talked about "the woman who does not feel forced to choose between a career and marriage, and is therefore free to find fulfillment in a combination of the two."

By the early 1960s, some women were beginning to make a few decisions as individuals, instead of doing things in traditional ways or just because society said they should. Gloria identified with this new choice-making and with new ideas about relationships with men. Her friendship with Bob Benton was based on the understanding that each of them was independent. She would not be giving up her career when they married, as many women of her mother's generation had done.

Gloria and Bob agreed to marry, but Gloria was hesitant. Did she have enough to offer in her own right? Was she ready to commit herself to one man? Did she still have to work on developing herself? They agreed to take one step at a time. First, they would apply for a marriage license, then they would buy the rings. The next step would be for Bob to buy a new suit, and Gloria a new dress. The rings had been purchased and the suit was hanging in Bob's closet, but Gloria waited. Finally, the marriage license expired.

Gloria had never been good about meeting her problems head-on, and Bob understood that by not choosing her wedding dress, Gloria was telling him she was not ready for marriage. Their marriage plans were dropped, but the two remained friends. Bob expanded his career to write and direct movies. Gloria gradually became well-known as a free-lance reporter. No longer associated with *Help!*, she sold ideas and articles to many magazines, eventually averaging up to $200 a week, a large amount in the 1960s.

Until this time, Gloria had been living in a tiny room in the northern part of New York City. Now she decided to move. She would share her new apartment with Barbara Nissim, an artist friend she had met through her work. Together they rented a large studio apartment on West Fifty-sixth Street, in the heart of the city. Enthusiastically, they carried their belongings up the three flights of stairs and divided the room in two.

Gloria's books, papers, and mementos of India occupied one side, and Barbara's paints, easel, and canvasses were on the other. Once Gloria's roll-top desk was set up with her typewriter on it, even the still-unpacked cartons could not spoil her sense of being at home.

At this point in her life, Gloria could look back at times both happy and sad. The death of her father in a car accident in California had been one of the sad times. At the funeral, surrounded by family, childhood recollections came back to her: Leo's jokes and laughter, his desire for adventure, the pleasure he took in being carefree. Her father was a man who enjoyed living without responsibility, a man who never wore a hat and never had a job. He used to say, "My office is in my hat"—the hat he never had.

Gloria had loved him and shared his sense of fun and his desire to be free. She, too, enjoyed not having a nine-to-five job, and her own office, although not in her hat, was a cluttered apartment. Her father had taught her to live with insecurity, and she found that she loved it. Gloria often said to her friends, "I wouldn't want to know how much money I'm going to earn next week, or that I'm going to have two weeks vacation a year." She was very much Leo Steinem's daughter, and once he was gone, there was an empty place in her heart.

But there had been many happy times, too, and many successes. With her growing reputation as a writer, Gloria had more assignments than she could handle. Although she had not yet succeeded in writing about

politics—women were rarely assigned to such subjects
in those days—editors were beginning to accept her
ideas, and now, in 1963, *Show* magazine asked Gloria
to go "undercover." Her assignment: to try and get a job
as a Playboy Bunny and then to describe to *Show*'s
readers what it was like.

The words "Playboy Bunny" hinted at the glamour
of big-city living, and the Bunnies were all attractive
young women. They worked as hostesses and wait-
resses at the Playboy Club, a semi-private men's club
that had branches in many large cities. The owner,
Hugh Hefner, was a wealthy magazine publisher who
had made his Playboy Club famous for its beautiful
women. The Playboy Bunnies were chosen for their
looks and were supposedly given the "chance of a lifetime." Many were said to have gone on to careers in
show business.

As she walked into the Playboy Club for her interview, Gloria wondered if she was pretty enough to be
accepted. But the woman in the personnel office had no
doubts, and after a week of training and studying the
"Bunny Bible," the Playboy Club's book of rules, Gloria was ready to work.

Squeezed into the briefest Bunny costume, the shoes
with the unfamiliar three-inch-high heels tight on her
feet, Gloria discovered that being a Playboy Bunny was
not the glamorous position that had been advertised.
She wondered if an interesting article and a byline with
Show magazine were worth this discomfort. The Bun-

nies worked harder than she had imagined, and the promised "big tips" did not materialize.

The average Bunny made less than $100 a week with salary and tips combined. Demerits for little things like a dirty tail—the piece of cotton fluff pinned on their costumes in imitation of a rabbit's tail—messy make-up, or eating on the job would result in deductions from a Bunny's salary. As Gloria learned about the job, she became more indignant about the working conditions. "You think differently in a sari," Gloria had said while in India. Now, she found that being dressed in the Bunny costume was also a very different experience. Gloria discovered that you feel very much at risk working with almost no clothes on.

The job had been advertised as exciting. Gloria only found hours of hard work, with no breaks and not even time to eat. The Bunnies were treated like children. There were rules about whom they could go out with, what they must wear, and how they should behave and talk with customers. After a week on the job, Gloria was still not used to carrying the heavy trays—or to being treated by the customers as an object for their personal amusement. "If you are my Bunny, can I take you home?" was the kind of remark that made her feel uncomfortable. She was glad when her last day of work came. Trying not to seem too happy, she told her supervisor that her mother was sick, so she did not know when she would return.

Gloria thought about what she would tell the editor

at *Show*. He had wanted her to write an amusing piece about the Playboy Club, but her article, she decided, could not be funny. She had gotten to know some of the Bunnies' problems: how the women were photographed for advertising purposes and never paid, how their tips had to be split with the management, and how they were pressured into going out with "special customers." She wanted to show the public that the Playboy Bunnies were real people.

Gloria's editor protested that people did not want to be troubled with the problems of others, but Gloria finally got her way. The article, entitled "A Bunny's Tale," was subtitled "*Show's* First Exposé for Intelligent People." It was published in two installments, in the May and June issues of 1963.

Although it was a well-written piece, the hope that Gloria had of making this article her stepping stone to more serious writing was not achieved. Now she was known as a Bunny, an image that didn't fit a serious writer. Only after feminism had helped her understand women's problems did she decide it had been worth it.

Chapter/Five

She wrote what she believed

Almost without realizing it, Gloria began making her way into the world of celebrities. She interviewed famous people for many magazines, and gradually became well-known herself.

Glamour magazine was one of the publications for which Gloria often worked. It featured articles on fashion, beauty, and travel, and interviews with well-known people. *Glamour*'s policy was occasionally to use their women writers as unpaid models in their articles on fashion, and Gloria was chosen as the *Glamour* girl for the February issue of 1964. One successful modeling experience led to another, and Gloria went to London to be photographed having her hair cut by Vidal Sassoon, a hairdresser who had become famous for his new styles. In London, she got not only a haircut, but an interview as well. Although, to Gloria's regret, *Glamour* was not interested in the more serious side of Mr.

Sassoon's life, that interview was a success and led to others.

James Baldwin, an outstanding black writer; John Lennon, one of the Beatles; and Mary Lindsay, wife of John Lindsay, mayor of New York City, were just a few of the famous people Gloria met and interviewed. She also wrote articles on the actor Michael Caine for *The New York Times Magazine* and on Dame Margot Fonteyn, the ballet dancer, for *McCall's*. For the *Ladies' Home Journal*, she interviewed a new young singer, Barbra Streisand, who was soon to become famous.

Years later, when she thought back on this list of important names, Gloria would say that she should have chosen more women like Pauline Fredericks, the television news reporter, or Barbara Walters, who did her own reporting on the "Today" show. These were two women about whom she had written. "I didn't fight hard enough," she would say. What she meant was that she should have featured more women who had been pioneers in broadcasting, or in other areas where women had once been excluded. But in the early 1960s, the recognition of women's abilities had not yet become an issue. Gloria worked to develop her own talents and use them as best she could.

In 1963 Gloria published *The Beach Book*, which included puzzles and games as well as serious reading. She worked with her publisher, Tom Guinzberg of Viking Press, and although the book was not the success they had hoped for, they became special friends.

Gloria also had a year of experience writing for TV with producer and writer Herb Sargent. Sargent was the producer of a new television comedy show based on the weekly news, to be called "That Was the Week That Was." He recruited writers and actors, and although Gloria had never written real comedy, except for a few skits back in college, she was ready for the challenge. She remembered with amusement both her parents' senses of humor and her father's ability to see the funny side in the occurrences of everyday life.

"What's on the radio?" Gloria would ask him, and he would joke, "There's a book on the radio," or something equally silly; the nonsense hidden in the sensible. When Gloria accepted Herb Sargent's offer and became one of the writers for "That Was the Week That Was," she used that kind of humor in her weekly feature called "Surrealism in Everyday Life."

The first segment of this unique comedy news show had aired on January 10, 1964. During its short run, Gloria learned a great deal from working closely with others. But many people did not like the program since it made fun of public figures and the government. It went off the air in May, 1965. By then, Gloria Steinem had gained status as a kind of celebrity herself. Not only was she interviewing others, but she was being interviewed. The *Washington Post* and *Glamour* wrote about her, as did her old hometown paper, the Toledo *Blade*. She was even interviewed on television.

With her confidence increased, Gloria took some

positive steps to enter into the world of politics. All her
life, she had been sympathetic with the poor and with
"people who were having a hard time." That was what
had led her to work for Adlai Stevenson in her high
school and college days. It was what had led her to
India, and now to the cause of a new leader, George
McGovern.

McGovern, a senator from South Dakota, was being discussed as a possible candidate for president of the
United States in 1968. Gloria first met him three years
before the election, in 1965, at a Boston airport. She had
been invited by her friends, John and Kitty Galbraith,
for a weekend of political talk in their Vermont home.
She and McGovern were supposed to drive up together.

During the car ride, Gloria had a chance to listen
and talk with McGovern about the war in Vietnam and
about President John Kennedy's ideas on foreign policy. McGovern had been a good friend of President
Kennedy before his tragic assassination in 1963, and
wanted to see Kennedy's policies continued.

After a weekend of political discussions at the Gal-
braiths' home, Gloria's favorable impression of George
McGovern was confirmed. She began writing about the
senator. Later, she would work to help him run for
president. That weekend was the beginning of many
years of serious political commitment for Gloria.

Thinking back on those days, Gloria felt her life was
"schizophrenic"—split in two—because she was not
writing about her real interests. She cared very much

about political issues like securing civil rights for black people in America, ending the war in Vietnam, helping the poor, and working to elect a president who cared about those things, too. What she got published were interviews with actors and actresses, background pieces about fashion, and lighthearted stories like her article on textured stockings for *The New York Times Magazine.*

Those years were the last of that divided part of her life. As she became more and more involved in politics, she was able to integrate her writing career and her concern with political issues. "Chance favors the prepared mind," she had once read. When a chance came, through a man named Clay Felker, Gloria was prepared to make the most of it.

Clay Felker had worked in publishing for many years and had been Gloria's editor at *Esquire.* Now he was ready to publish a magazine of his own. He wanted his magazine to appeal to New Yorkers and people from other cities who were intelligent, sophisticated, and interested in both politics and the arts. He planned to call it simply *New York*, and he wanted Gloria to be a part of it.

Gloria joined forces with Clay from the very beginning by helping him raise money for his magazine. Then, when the staff was being organized, she became an editor—one of the people who would not only write for the magazine, but decide what kinds of articles would be printed. For herself, Gloria knew, there would be no more interviews with starlets or articles on fashion. She would interview presidential candidates, senators, and ambassadors—leaders who made a difference in New York City and in the nation.

From its very first issue, in July, 1968, *New York* was a success, and "City Politic," the political column that Gloria named and often wrote for, became well-known. Gloria began to be considered one of the writers who could influence what people thought about a politician. After she wrote about Richard Nixon, the 1968 Republican candidate for president, many felt that she was partly responsible for people's misgivings about him. When she turned to the Democratic Party and began to examine the many candidates who wanted to be president, others became angry. One of them was Eugene McCarthy, a man she had once supported. Her article about him, called "Learning to Love Eugene," was said to have contributed to disillusionment with this man who was once the hope of the Peace Movement.

In spite of the fact that some people disliked the way she used the power of her typewriter, Gloria herself did not feel powerful. She wrote what she believed, and although she was often distressed when people became angry at her, she continued her work. She loved her job with *New York* magazine. The office was busy and exciting; it was a place where things happened. Besides giving her the chance to write about politics, *New York* gave Gloria her first opportunity to be an on-the-scene reporter who could cover the news while it was happening.

In April of 1968, Martin Luther King, Jr. was shot and killed. King was the most important black civil rights leader in America, and was loved and admired by many blacks and whites. After the announcement of his death, some blacks in a few cities began to riot, and New Yorkers waited and worried. Would there be riots in their city, too?

People were beginning to gather in the streets of Harlem, a black neighborhood in New York City. They were angry and upset and might begin rioting at any time. Clay Felker picked up the phone and called Gloria.

"Get up to Harlem," he told her, "and just talk to the people. We want to know what is happening there."

Gloria went as quickly as she could. Of course it was dangerous for a young woman to enter an area where riots might erupt at any minute, but Gloria did not feel afraid. She remembered her experience traveling in India during troubled times, and knew that safety meant staying close to other women. That is what she did. At the end of a long night of talking to the citizens of Harlem, and to political leaders who had come out to try to calm the people, Gloria was able to report that all was quiet. There had been no injury or damage.

This would not be the only time that Gloria took risks to cover a story or to stand up for what she believed. Just a few months later, attending the Demo-

cratic National Convention of 1968 as a volunteer for
McGovern, she faced similar dangers. Many students
and other young people had come to the Democratic
political convention in Chicago to try and convince the
delegates to choose a candidate who would be against
the Vietnam War. They were eager to make an impression, but most of the candidates ignored them. In an
attempt to make themselves heard, the students took
to the streets carrying signs and chanting slogans for
peace.

The Chicago police were angry and distrustful of the
students. Determined to keep order in the city, they
reacted to disorders before they even began, advancing
into the crowds with clubs ready. Before very long a real
riot had erupted. Gloria, watching it happen right before her eyes, was amazed to see groups of police offi-
cers going after civilians and beating them. When the
rioting finally ended, a large number of students were
hurt and others were in jail. Many Americans were
shocked at what had happened and disappointed by the
behavior of the Chicago police. "I lost my sense that the
police protect you," Gloria said after that event.

Gloria returned from the convention with more understanding of how the political process works. Although her candidate, George McGovern, did not win
the nomination, Gloria continued her commitment to
the many causes in which they both believed. One of
these causes was help for working people, especially
those who were being taken advantage of unfairly.

Gloria had been poor when she was young, and could identify with people who were fighting for a better life.

While still working for *New York*, she heard about the farm workers in California. They were trying to get support to organize a grape boycott. What they wanted was to convince the people of America to stop buying grapes until the farm bosses agreed to pay the farm workers a fair wage. Cesar Chavez, the leader of the boycott, had sent his followers throughout the country to try and raise money for their cause. That was how Gloria met a woman named Marian Moses.

Marian arrived in New York with a small suitcase and only five dollars in her pocket. She knew about Gloria through a friend in California, and asked for her help. First, Gloria took Marian into her home, then she began to listen to what she had to say about the farm workers' lives and their problems. Gloria was impressed with Marian's talents as an organizer—how she went about raising money and establishing a support group. "She could organize an ice cube," Gloria said about her new friend. "She organized me."

Gloria joined Marian Moses' cause, and again set out to work for what she believed. She eventually traveled to California to join the farm workers and their families in a dramatic Poor People's March to the Mexican border. Gloria's job was to arrange for press coverage during that march.

The weather was hot and dusty in Southern California, and the march was difficult. Many people in Amer-

ica were against the boycott. It was not easy to convince
the newspapers that they should write about this group
of poor people, many of whom could not even speak
English, and Gloria worked hard to explain their mis-
sion to the press. When it was over, she returned to New
York with a sense of accomplishment—and an interview with Cesar Chavez which she had previously obtained for *Look* magazine.

Gloria did not find out until much later that *Look*
did not want to publish her article at first. The grape
boycott and the man who organized it were controver-
sial, and the publishers were uncomfortable featuring
the topic in their magazine. Pat Carbine, Gloria's friend
and managing editor of *Look*, fought for Gloria and for
what she had written. Pat felt so strongly about including Gloria's piece that she threatened to quit her job
if the magazine publishers did not print it. Gloria's
article did get into *Look* magazine in April, 1969, but
Pat Carbine didn't tell Gloria how difficult it had been.
Gloria only found out much later, when she and Pat
became co-workers on a new venture.

Chapter/Six

The voices were all women's voices

Seated in her new office, which was already cluttered with books, letters, and papers, Gloria looked around and saw the bustle and activity of a busy magazine staff. In appearance it was not very different from the offices at *New York* magazine or any other monthly publication, except for one thing: these offices were filled with women. The voices she heard talking on the phone, discussing editorial policy, and calling out to each other across partitions were all women's voices. It was 1972, and this was the office of *Ms.* magazine—the first national magazine to be completely run and controlled by women. The magazine's purpose was to address the true problems of women. No fashion pages, recipes, or tips on make-up would appear; instead, there were articles on working and managing a home, relationships with husbands, women's medical and sexual problems, and getting an education. *Ms.* carried news about the new feminist movement that had swept the country since 1970 and was beginning to affect many women.

It had taken Gloria a long time to realize that, as a woman, the problems of other women were important to her. She had come to know that politics involved not only presidential elections and votes in Congress, but also how families were run. She felt that if the family itself were not a democracy, with rights for women and children, it was impossible to train people for democracy outside the family.

This realization had first come to Gloria in 1969 when abortion hearings were being held by a committee of the New York State legislature. At the hearings, fourteen male legislators and one nun testified for or against women's right to decide this issue as individuals. In her column for *New York*, Gloria covered a separate protest meeting held in a church basement. There, she listened to women tell their own stories. They talked about the difficulties of having an abortion. Many had suffered serious injury from an illegal abortion given under unsanitary conditions.

It was not difficult for Gloria to identify with these women. She, too, had been forced to seek an abortion when she was only twenty-two, and shuddered to think how different her life might have been if she had not been able to do so. She remembered clearly her own feelings of desperation and shame. In that basement hearing room, she began to see that she shared those feelings and that experience with thousands of women.

Later, Gloria took the first step towards making people understand what a widespread problem illegal abortion was. In 1972 she publicly discussed her abortion, and invited all others who had also had abortions to stand up and be counted. Many women did, among them women whose names were widely known and respected. Each signed her name to a petition to admit that she had once done something illegal. Every woman who signed believed that abortion should become legal, and was asking that the law be changed. A year later, in 1973, it became legal throughout the United States.

The 1969 abortion hearings in New York had electrified Gloria. She began to read about the new feminist philosophy and to view her own life—and her mother's—in light of what she had learned. "I finally understood," Gloria was to write later, "why I identify with 'out' groups. I belong to one, too."

How different Ruth's and Gloria's lives would have been, she realized, if her mother's life and work had been valued as much as a man's. If it had, Ruth's family might not have ignored her illness for so long and allowed her to waste her life and her talents. If they saw her as important, they might have found help for her. Perhaps it was too late for her own mother, but the women's rights movement might help thousands of other women to achieve all that they could.

Right after the abortion hearings, Gloria did additional research on the women's movement and wrote an article for *New York* magazine titled "After Black

Power, Women's Liberation." The article won the Penney-Missouri Journalism Award as one of the first reports in a national magazine on the new feminism. Gloria began to focus on feminists and their writing and to write article after article on the movement.

Gloria also was one of thousands of women who marched through the center of New York City in the Women's Strike for Equality, a rally to celebrate women's gaining of the vote. Gloria began to understand the idea of "sisterhood" as she met other women from all walks of life, each ready to work for the ideals of equality for all people.

The belief that women were as important as men, and that both men and women had to be helped to understand that, led Gloria to one of the biggest challenges of her life. One day she interviewed Dorothy Pitman Hughes. Dorothy was a black woman, a founder and director of a community day care center. During the interview, a young man who was about to be married began speaking with them. He said he did not want his wife to continue to work after their marriage. Both Gloria and Dorothy disagreed with him and set out to explain to him that his wife's talent should not be disregarded—that she had a responsibility to herself as well as to her new husband. Their arguments convinced the young man, and he agreed that his wife must be given the same chances that he would have.

Gloria and Dorothy looked at each other, both thinking the same thing. If they could convince one person to see things differently, they could convince others: not one or two at a time, but hundreds at a time.

Although Gloria liked people and was perfectly at ease in small groups and private conversations, the thought of saying the very same things in front of an audience of hundreds of people filled her with dread. She felt she could never do it. But Dorothy encouraged her, and so did other friends.

Gloria remembered Robert Kennedy, brother of the late president, John Kennedy, and a presidential candidate himself before his murder. Gloria had admired him more than any politician she had met. He was one of the shyest people she knew, Gloria would recall later, but he had spoken out because he cared about helping and changing the country. Gloria cared about women's rights. She decided that she could and would overcome her nervousness and fear.

Before Gloria knew it, an agent had arranged some speaking dates for her and Dorothy Pitman Hughes: a team of women, one white and one black, who would be able to appeal to all kinds of women. Although her knees shook and her hands trembled as she gripped the sheet of paper with her notes on it, Gloria stood up to address each audience before her. With Dorothy's support, she managed her first speech with no major disasters, and over the next months of speaking gradually lost her fear. Continued tips from Dorothy, a more experienced speaker, plus favorable responses from their audiences made Gloria more sure of herself. She would continue giving lectures for five years. First teamed with Dorothy, she later toured with two other black friends: Florynce Kennedy, a lawyer, and then with Margaret Sloan, a writer and activist from Chicago.

Although she never felt completely comfortable as a public speaker, convincing people and explaining the importance of her ideas eventually became more important to Gloria than her own feelings. "I saw a whole population of women who desperately wanted information," Gloria later explained. The women came to listen and learn, but their questions taught Gloria many things about what the women of America needed and how they felt. Those questions, and many letters concerning everything from starting a child care center to going back to school led her to help start the Women's Action Alliance.

The Women's Action Alliance was an organization that developed educational programs and services to assist women and women's organizations. Another Alliance founder was Brenda Feigen, who also believed that women needed practical help. With Gloria, she worked to make the Alliance a reality. One of the Alliance's first projects was helping parents bring up and educate boys and girls equally, instead of assuming that boys were always good at certain things and girls at other things. They also tried to help increase women's economic opportunities.

Some of the Alliance women began thinking that they could develop a newsletter or even a national magazine. Meetings were held in Gloria's apartment, and soon plans began to be formed.

Among the planners of the new magazine were women who would become important contributors to the magazine and the feminist movement: Jane O'Reilly, Cathy O'Hair, Letty Cottin Pogrebin, Joanne Edgar, Mary Peacock, Florynce Kennedy, and many others. All of them came from different backgrounds, races, and religions, but all were committed to the new magazine. They would call it *Ms.* The word "Ms." had become the symbol of the liberated woman who was identified not by her marital status, but by what she herself did and could accomplish.

The women were ready to work hard to make *Ms.* a reality, but first, they needed money to publish the magazine. They began fundraising for the new venture. Although some of the people they approached were enthusiastic, most felt that a feminist magazine was too big a risk. As 1971 was coming to an end, prospects for funding *Ms.* magazine seemed bleak.

Then Clay Felker, Gloria's friend and boss at *New York* magazine, made a suggestion. Once each year, in December, *New York* published a supplement to their regular features and articles. They needed a theme for this year's supplement. Would Gloria like to compile a first issue of her new women's magazine and allow it to be part of the December issue? If Gloria and the other editors did the work for free, Clay would finance its printing and production. Then, if it was a success, money would come.

It sounded like a wonderful chance to put a test copy of *Ms.* on the market, and all the women agreed. On December 20, 1971, just before the new year, *New York* magazine came out. The women's supplement was a big success! Additional articles were added to the supplement to form a preview issue of *Ms.*, which was distributed in January, 1972.

Gloria was in California doing publicity for that preview issue when television reviewers began calling her and asking why *Ms.* was not at their newsstands. Afraid that *Ms.* had never been delivered, Gloria quickly checked with the offices in New York and with the California magazine distributors. Yes, it had indeed been sent and delivered. The first issue had been sold out before morning!

Gloria would later remember that discovery as one of the high points in her life. *Ms.* magazine was not only what she and a handful of her associates wanted; it was what hundreds of thousands of women in America had been waiting for.

Chapter/Seven

We won't be told what to do anymore

Gloria began to be more and more involved with the feminist movement. The issues of women's rights, she was finding, were so much a part of life that they could not be separated from any aspect of it. She had already discovered that politics began in the family structure and spread into the community, the city, the state, and the nation. Gloria felt that none of these areas should be neglected. The Women's Action Alliance, which she had helped establish in 1971, concentrated on educating children equally, so that boys would not have an educational advantage over girls, either in families or in schools. But Gloria could see many other areas where women did not get fair representation in society. One of the most obvious of these was in legislatures and other governing bodies throughout the country. In the early 1970s, few women held state or federal offices. Feminists pointed out that women could influence greatly the laws in each city and community by taking part in the lawmaking process. That meant that pro-equality women had to be elected as representatives, senators, and committee leaders.

Women began to work towards this goal by organizing the National Women's Political Caucus. Founded in July, 1971, by a group of women led by Congresswomen Bella Abzug and Shirley Chisholm of New York, and Patsy Mink of Hawaii, the organization saw its purpose as the election and appointment of pro-equality women. Gloria was involved in this new group, too. She saw its founding as a major accomplishment, and one that fit her longtime interest in national politics. Although she didn't consider herself primarily an organizer, Gloria did feel confident of her talents as a writer. It was she who worded the guiding principles for the National Women's Political Caucus after its goals had been worked out in an all-night session in Washington, D.C. She had done the same for the Women's Action Alliance, and would do it in the future for the many other groups she was to help establish.

It was Gloria who chose the phrase "reproductive freedom" at this time. This was the right to decide whether or not to have a baby. Besides making birth control information and methods available, reproductive freedom included the choice to have a safe and legal abortion and the right to decent health care if a woman did choose to have a child. Feminists felt these were part of their constitutional rights. Establishing reproductive freedom was included in the caucus' statement of purpose, as were statements against racism and against violence as an acceptable means of solving conflicts.

The first test for the Women's Political Caucus came with the 1972 Democratic National Convention. The women wanted reproductive freedom to be a plank in the party's platform—the official list of Democrats' beliefs and goals. Before the convention began, Gloria, along with a group of women from the caucus, met with Senator George McGovern (now a serious presidential contender) about it. When they asked for his support, he hesitated. Later, he allowed a statement about reproductive freedom to be taken out of his platform by a woman advisor.

Gloria was disappointed, but she and other women were more determined than ever to bring up women's issues at this convention. One young woman delegate got enough signatures on a petition to introduce the issue of reproductive freedom as a minority plank at the convention. That meant that it would be decided on the convention floor anyway, in spite of lack of support from the major candidates. "It's the strength of the women's movement," Gloria thought with satisfaction. "Some of us won't be told what to do anymore, not even by each other."

Gloria herself had come to the Democratic Convention as a spokesperson for the Women's Political Caucus. She had run as a delegate for Shirley Chisholm, a black woman and representative from New York who

was running for president of the United States, but
McGovern delegates had been elected instead.

McGovern had been surprised at Gloria's support
of Chisholm, since Gloria had supported him for so
many years. But Gloria felt that even though Shirley
Chisholm had little chance of winning, being a black
and a woman, her candidacy would help make voters
aware of the needs of minority groups and of wom-
en's abilities. As Gloria had explained in an article for
Look magazine early in 1970, a woman president was
needed so that people would not "go on supposing the
current social order reflects some natural order." The
only thing that will convince people that a woman can
be president, Gloria believed, is to elect one, or at
least to nominate one.

The convention was exciting, and very different
from the one four years earlier in Chicago which had
been marked by rioting and bloodshed. This time the
women, under the leadership of the Women's Political
Caucus, were organized and ready. They won fights
to allow more women in each state's delegation, helped
get a woman elected as the co-chair at the convention,
and introduced a women's plank to be voted on by the
delegates. Finally, after McGovern was chosen as the
presidential candidate from the Democratic Party, they
even managed to push for a woman candidate, Frances
"Sissy" Farenthold of Texas, for vice president. Although Farenthold lost to Senator Thomas Eagleton,
who was McGovern's own choice, the women had put

up a good fight—she came in second, winning over several other male candidates.

The battles for power at the Miami convention were often frightening for the women. Most of them had never been involved in this kind of rough political give-and-take before. They faced not only possible failure, but ridicule and criticism because of their inexperience. Despite their fears, they worked hard to have the women's plank passed by the convention and, with the exception of reproductive rights, they succeeded. After it was over, Gloria, thinking about what had been done, could not help but compare it to previous national conventions, where there had been hardly any women delegates and no mention of women's problems in the party platform. Referring to this landmark convention, Gloria would later write that "women are never again going to be mindless coffee-makers or mindless policy-makers in politics. . . .We have to learn to lead ourselves."

Gloria was learning. Among other things, she had learned that no one would speak for women's issues if women did not, and that most male candidates, even if they were sincerely concerned with women's rights, would not understand the real problems unless women explained them. Gloria saw herself as a writer who could put "common feelings into words." As a speaker on women's issues, a representative to political conventions, a founder of organizations to serve women's needs, and now one of the editors of a major women's magazine, she had many chances to explain the new feminist position by using everyday examples that people could understand.

Also in 1972, *McCall's* magazine named Gloria Steinem "Woman of the Year." She was interviewed, quoted, photographed, and investigated. To Gloria's surprise, a young feminist reporter and researcher even taught her things about her own family. She had known that her father's mother was Pauline Steinem, and had come to America from Russian-controlled Poland as a young woman. Yet she had never learned that "Mama Einey," as she and Sue called her, had been an important suffragist—a woman who fought for women's right to vote back in the early part of the twentieth century. Gloria discovered that Grandmother Pauline had spoken before the Women's Suffrage Commission and the United States Senate on behalf of women's right to vote. She had been the first woman elected to the Board of Education of Toledo, Ohio, in 1904; was a delegate to the International Convention of Women, held in Switzerland in 1908; and served as president of the Ohio Women's Suffrage Association from 1908 to 1911.

Gloria was proud to have a grandmother who had been a pioneer in women's rights. But, she wondered, how could this brave and intelligent woman have failed to help Ruth, her son's wife, during the early years of her mental illness? Many years later, when writing openly about her mother's problems, Gloria explained that, although her grandmother had fought for women's right to vote, "she had never changed the politics of her own life." She had not been able to change the way she had been taught to act towards her husband and her four sons. "My grandmother was a public feminist and a private isolationist," Gloria wrote. She felt that her grandmother had never connected her politics and her home life. Ruth Steinem had needed more help than just the right to vote and to work. Gloria, understanding that, committed herself more and more to organizations and associations created to answer women's needs.

Another organization which Gloria helped establish was the Ms. Foundation for Women. It was dedicated to helping women by granting money to support grass-roots, self-help projects of women's groups and individuals throughout America. Working with Gloria on this project were her co-workers from *Ms.* magazine, Pat Carbine and Letty Cottin Pogrebin.

Also included in Ms. Foundation planning was an enthusiastic young feminist and actress, Marlo Thomas. With the help of Letty Cottin Pogrebin, and children's stories from the pages of *Ms.*, she had created a children's television show and a record which explained, through songs and examples from everyday life, that boys and girls have equal talents and capabilities and can do the same things in the world. The record later became a book, and a stage version was performed live in schools. It was called "Free to Be

You and Me," and the ideas it introduced were used throughout the country as an educational tool. Thomas and all who worked on those projects contributed the profits to the new Ms. Foundation for Women.

The Coalition of Labor Union Women was another group which Gloria helped to form. The coalition tried to help women who felt they were not getting a fair deal within their own unions, or who wanted to organize new labor unions. In 1974 she went to Chicago as one of its founding members, seeing this organization as an important part of women's struggle for equal work, and as another way to fight for an end to discrimination against women in all kinds of jobs.

The 1970s were busy years, and happy ones. Without even realizing how much time had gone by, Gloria sailed into her fortieth year. She looked young and felt even younger. "You don't look forty," one reporter said at her birthday celebration. Gloria laughed and answered: "This is what forty looks like. We've been lying for so long, who would know?" Women often feel that growing older is not good, because it might make them less valued by the men in their lives. Gloria believed differently and wanted to change the ideas of others. She didn't lie about her age, because she felt it didn't matter how old you were—only what you could accomplish.

Each year Gloria added new accomplishments and new friends. In 1975 she met a very special man, Stanley Pottinger. Pottinger was a lawyer who lived and worked in Washington, D.C., where he headed the Civil Rights Division of the Justice Department. Gloria was first introduced to him when he flew to New York to talk about sex discrimination cases being prepared by the government. The two found themselves working together closely and sharing ideas.

Gloria felt that Stan was one of the few men she had ever met who seemed to understand the problems that women face. He cared not only about Gloria herself, but about the women's movement and its goals and ideals. He shared her commitment to equality for women, and with Gloria, actively supported the amendment guaranteeing women's rights, the Equal Rights Amendment (ERA). This proposed change to the United States Constitution was to be voted on in many states within the next few years. Stan had been married and divorced. Raising two small children himself made him aware of many kinds of problems faced by women. He brought all that experience and understanding to his new relationship with Gloria. Stan agreed with what she had written in 1970: "Men and women [must] progress together or not at all."

Gloria found herself traveling to Washington more and more often to spend time with Stan. Although she was as busy as ever, she made time to be with her new friend. She looked forward to closing the door of her tiny, crowded office at *Ms.*, rushing to the airport, and taking the hour shuttle flight to Washington.

Gloria's interests during those years were varied.

Her involvement in politics continued and she was appointed to the platform committee of the Democratic National Committee. There was work with the Women's Action Alliance, and their renewed attack on discrimination against women in employment. Gloria was writing about sisterhood, demonstrating against pornography, interviewing candidates, and continuing the fight for equal rights for all women. There was much work still to be done.

Gloria as a Playboy Bunny. In 1964 she got a job as a waitress at a Playboy Club, and wrote about the experience for Show *magazine.*

Dorothy Pitman Hughes (left) with Gloria. The pair toured the country as a speaking team, giving talks on equality between men and women.

Gloria relaxing in her New York City apartment, where she has lived for many years.

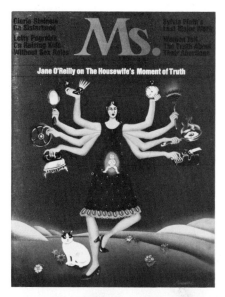

The first issue of Ms. *magazine, which appeared on newsstands in January, 1972.*

The original staff of Ms. *magazine in 1972. Gloria (second row, fourth from left) was one of the founding editors of this national magazine—the first major publication to be wholly created and controlled by women.*

Covers from four of the magazines featuring articles on Gloria Steinem. During the 1970s, she became one of the most well-known spokespersons for the feminist movement.

Gloria (right) with Letty Cottin Pogrebin (left) a co-founder and editor at Ms. *and Marlo Thomas (center), an actress who produced "Free to Be. . .You and Me," a non-sexist, multi-racial children's record album.*

Gloria with Stan, Paul, and Katie Pottinger at the ERA Extension March held July 9, 1978, in Washington, D.C. Organizers hoped that this event would demonstrate popular support for the ERA and convince Congress to extend the deadline for its ratification.

(Top) *Gloria takes on President Jimmy Carter's administration in a* Ms. *maga-zine article entitled "Carter Discovers Life is Unfair."*
(Bottom) *Gloria (left) with actress Loretta Swit (center) and publisher Pat Carbine (right) at a 1982 party celebrating the tenth anniversary of the founding of* Ms. *magazine.*

Gloria with her mother, Ruth Steinem. Ruth went to her daughter's lectures whenever possible and enjoyed Gloria's success. She had recovered enough in her later years to lead a fuller life.

Chapter/Eight

To humanize society

The United Nations declared 1975 International Women's Year. It was to be the year when the world would examine and address universal problems of women: not only equal rights and equal pay, but women's special problems with hunger, nutrition, child care, and birth control. These issues were especially pressing in Third World countries (the name given to the underdeveloped nations of Africa, Asia, and South America), where hunger was widespread and women were often treated poorly. The International Women's Year promised to be a major step forward for the consciousness of women's rights. It would be highlighted by a conference in Mexico City, which was to be attended by delegates from all over the world.

The United States' thirty-nine delegates had been appointed by President Richard Nixon and by his successor, President Gerald Ford. Gloria was not chosen as a delegate, but she and many other individual women and groups would be in Mexico City anyway. As one of the leading woman writers in the United States, she had been the only Western journalist invited to speak before a group of Third World reporters at the pre-conference. She looked forward to meeting the delegates and attending some of the many workshops.

Women from 123 countries began to assemble in Mexico City by the beginning of June, and the conference officially opened on June 18, 1975. Thousands of women and men whose skin tones and hair color ranged from fair Scandinavian to dark African, many wearing the national dress of their countries, had come together. They were hoping to improve the lives of women throughout the world.

The conference lasted for one week. During that time there were speeches, workshops, and discussions on a range of topics, from caring for newborn babies to education and women's roles in religion and politics. It was in the area of politics that the conference ran into trouble. Gloria, although she did not attend the conference itself, had hoped, along with many others, that women could overcome bitter differences of belief and concentrate on areas of mutual concern. However, they soon realized that there were groups who could not put aside their own countries' self-interest, and who attempted to use the International Women's Conference as a forum for propaganda.

The American delegates complained as individuals

and as a group, but could do nothing to change the direction of the conference. "The true issues, the problems of women, are being forgotten here," said Carole de Saram, president of the New York branch of the National Organization for Women. She sadly noted "a rift [split] between women from rich and poor lands" which had succeeded in drowning out those who were seeking more unity. The U.N. Women's Conference had turned into just another political confrontation.

Some women also claimed that the meeting concentrated "on political issues that represent the male mentality." Before the conference ended, it passed resolutions with which the U.S. delegates could not agree, especially one which condemned Zionism, the national movement of the Jewish people to have their own country, as a form of racism. Delegates returned to the United States disappointed and saddened. "Some American and other feminists," commented the *New York Times* on June 24, 1975, "have denounced the conference as a male-organized, male-dominated attempt to co-opt [take over] women's issues."

Gloria, too, was disappointed with the conference. She felt that the only thing it had done was allow some women to connect with each other in spite of all the controversy. There had been little progress toward solving the real problems of the world's women. Although additional International Women's Conferences had been scheduled for 1980 and 1985, marking out a "Decade of Women," many were doubtful that those other conferences would be any different from this one.

Gloria felt more hopeful that things could change in the United States. She wanted to reach out to every woman who was tired of the belief that "violence is an inevitable [sure-to-happen] or acceptable way of solving conflicts." A few years earlier she had urged that the aim of the women's movement should be "to humanize society by bringing the values of women's culture into it; not simply to put individual women in men's places." In order to accomplish that goal, women had to have equal rights. Gloria continued fighting for a major piece of legislation, the Equal Rights Amendment.

This proposed amendment to the Constitution had been presented to Congress many times since it had first been introduced in 1923. Congress finally passed the amendment in 1972, but gave it only seven years to be approved by enough states to make it law. Gloria was in the forefront of the battle to have the Equal Rights Amendment ratified by individual states. She wrote about equal rights; spoke about the idea in televised debates, interviews, and lectures; and helped to raise money. "It is only fair and just," she insisted. For Gloria, it was as simple as that.

Beginning in 1974, *Ms.* magazine had found another way to present women's issues and fight for the ERA. It started and sponsored a show called "Woman Alive!" on public television. Gloria was its host, interviewing ordinary women and presenting new women performers.

Gloria's very first work as a television host had been several years before in Canada. She had been terribly nervous and frightened then, and had chosen Canada because she had no friends there to watch her. Since that time, she had gotten more experience as a public speaker and had made many TV guest appearances in the United States. Her first chance in America to host an interview show had been in 1972, when the first issue of *Ms.* magazine had just been produced. That year David Frost, a noted journalist and TV personality from England, had turned over one of his shows to Gloria so that she could interview some of the women active in feminist causes. That show had been a success, so its basic format was copied for "Woman Alive!"

Each week on the show, Gloria, her long, straight hair brushing her shoulders, walked out onto the set to introduce her guests to the viewers. The jeans and turtleneck tops she wore looked good on her, and many young women copied the style of her aviator-type glasses. She had become a trendsetter in looks as well as ideas.

While the fight for the ERA went on, American women would have another chance to address issues which had been overlooked in Mexico City at the U.N. conference. Bella Abzug had fought to have the United States set aside $5 million of government funds for a series of women's conferences in each of the states, plus one national meeting so that women could set their own agenda. Now, President Jimmy Carter wanted to show

an interest in women's issues. He announced that Abzug, one of the women most active in the feminist
movement, would head a national commission to super-
vise and organize the American Conference on Wom-
en. Besides Abzug, Carter named forty other women to
this national commission, including Gloria Steinem.

Helping to set up the individual state conferences,
where delegates would be chosen for the national convention, was one of Gloria's tasks for the commission.
The delegates were supposed to represent the ranges of
age, race, income level, religion, and ethnic background
of women in each state.

At many state conferences, groups opposed to equality for women often attempted to take charge of the
meetings and direct or block the choosing of delegates.
These groups objected to all the goals of the women's
movement and felt that women should keep their traditional role in the home. They tried to elect delegates
who would represent that point of view. In spite of
these disagreements, however, representatives were chosen from each state for a women's congress. It was
to be held in Houston, Texas, from November 18
through November 21, 1977, and the recommendations
passed by it would be sent to the United States Congress for possible action.

Those were exciting times for Gloria. She traveled
from state to state speaking with women from all walks
of life. She had done this many times before, when she
had been on speaking tours and talked about the new

she knew. Even though her sister Sue was always sympathetic, she could do very little.

It was just then, when things seemed as bad as they could be, that an offer came from the church next door to buy their house. Sue was told of the offer, too, and it set her to thinking. She telephoned Gloria with a plan in mind: if Leo took care of Ruth, Gloria could move to Washington. She would live with Sue, finish her senior year, and then, she hoped, go to college.

"He will never agree!" Gloria had warned Sue. Nevertheless, a ray of hope had entered her mind. Maybe there *was* a solution.

Sue contacted their father, scheduled a vacation from her own job, and arranged a family conference. On a summer morning in 1951, Leo, Sue, and Gloria met together in Toledo. Over breakfast they discussed the problems of Ruth and the house. Sue proposed her plan, explaining that they could accept the offer made by the church next door to them and sell the house. Ruth would stay with Leo, and Gloria would come to Washington with her. When Sue had finished, Leo said, "I can't do it. How can I care for Ruth when I have to travel and make a living?"

Gloria had heard those words many years ago, when her father had left. Even though she knew it was true, and believed that her father had done the best he could, her heart sank with disappointment.

Breakfast was over and nothing had been settled. Leo offered to drive Gloria to Petrie's, the women's clothing store where she worked as a salesgirl. As the car stopped in front of the store, Gloria was suddenly overcome with a feeling of hopelessness and burst into tears.

Gloria's father was shocked. He had not seen her cry since she was a baby. He loved his daughter and knew how hard it had been for her to care for her mother. Leo groped for a solution. Would Sue's suggestion make such a difference? Perhaps it would.

Before she knew what had happened, Gloria, still crying, felt her father's arms around her, and heard him say surprising words: "Okay, I'll do it. For one year; only one year, and then I'm bringing her back."

At seventeen, one year seemed like a lifetime to Gloria. Her father had given her the gift she most wanted, and Sue's idea transformed the coming year— her last before college—into a carefree time such as she had not known before.

feminist movement, but now there was a special purpose. This women's convention was a kind of constitutional convention for women, where they could speak for themselves and ask for new federal laws. These laws would address women's needs and problems.

"Beware of news reports from Houston that concentrate on individual celebrities," advised an article in the November, 1977, issue of *Ms*. The real action at the national conference, that writer felt, would be "with the Kentucky coal-miners' widows, the black trade union women from Chicago, homemakers' rights advocates, and the other hard-working, little-known delegates." Gloria found that prediction to be true. Known for her longtime commitment to the poor and disadvantaged, she felt a special pride when she was asked to be the scribe for an historic alliance of minority women's groups. There were black and Hispanic women, Asian and native American women. Such a diverse group of women had never met before.

Getting their resolution passed on the convention floor took hours of hard work and behind-the-scenes convincing. Negotiating in Houston taught many women how to make politics work for them, a skill they would later need in working for the causes in which they believed. When the minority plank won by a unanimous vote, Gloria remembered that final victory as another high point in her life.

When the Women's Convention at Houston was over, and the votes tallied, a long list of resolutions was sent to President Carter for further action by the Congress. Now it would be up to the United States government to decide whether they would follow the women's suggestions or not. Many were doubtful of any action by Congress; others hoped for the best. But as Gloria and the other women returned home, they understood that even if not one of their resolutions became the law of the land, they were still winners. They had met new allies, learned new skills, and gained new understanding that would help them to continue the fight.

Soon after the convention, Gloria went to Washington to study on a Woodrow Wilson Fellowship from the Smithsonian Institution. It would pay her while she spent a year researching the effects of feminism on political theory. She took a leave of absence from full-time work at *Ms.* to become a scholar, although she continued to write and edit for *Ms.* on weekends. After so many years of activism, a year doing research was appealing. In addition, being in Washington would give her more opportunity to spend time with her mother and sister, and with Stan.

Ruth Steinem had been better for many years since her early hospitalization. She had lived in her own apartment near Sue and led a more active life, participating in community and church affairs. But now she was older and in poor health, and needed the support of both Gloria and Sue. Gloria looked forward to the times she could spend with her family in Washington, and to the challenge of the year ahead.

Chapter/Nine

A long process for full equality

"Writing that leads to action," Gloria wrote, "may be just as important in the long run as much of the fact and fiction published in conventional [ordinary] ways."

Gloria had often thought of writing a book, and was sorry that she hadn't kept a diary while on her many speaking tours. She sometimes looked back with regret on the long hours she had spent just writing fund-raising letters, or jotting notes for her next speech. The Woodrow Wilson Fellowship promised Gloria the chance she needed to write that book.

Yet, when the year was up, her book would be far from ready, and Gloria would still be leading such an active, busy life that she had little time to make future plans or take on long-term projects. Each month, it seemed, new issues demanded her attention. She had to evaluate each issue and decide how much time to devote to it. She also had to decide whether her speaking out on an issue would make a difference in resolving it. Friends admired her dedication to "giving and measuring her energies according to how many people she could help," but that dedication took a great deal of effort and energy.

One of Gloria's major interests in 1978 continued to be the passage of the Equal Rights Amendment. It was very close to becoming law—only three more states needed to ratify the amendment—but the struggle continued. Supporters of the amendment watched its progress as it came up for a vote in each state. They began to see that a large opposition was forming. Virginia voted against the ERA. Then Kentucky, a state that had previously passed the amendment, changed its mind and voted to rescind it, even though this was not really binding. Time was running out. The deadline for passage was March, 1979, only a year away, and unless the allowed time was extended, the ERA would fail and have to be introduced in Congress all over again.

An important test of the amendment was to be in the state of Illinois. Feminists there were working hard to convince the Illinois legislators to vote yes. They were confident of victory, but on June 9, 1978, when the vote was counted in the Illinois House of Representatives, the ERA was defeated. It came up for a second vote just two weeks later, and was defeated again, in spite of the hard work of so many. Without this additional state's ratification, hopes for passage of the ERA by the following year looked dim.

Gloria had followed the ERA countdown as the bill had been considered in one state legislature after another. *Ms.* magazine, too, had kept its readers informed on the results of each state's vote. Feminists started using both positive and negative means to encourage passage of the ERA. A boycott had begun early in the year. Women refused to buy products, travel, or schedule meetings in states which had not yet passed the Equal Rights Amendment. The National Organization for Women (NOW) had declared a "state of emergency." Said the NOW women, "We are determined to be victorious [because] we will not tolerate the possibility of living lives in which there is no realistic hope of sisters and brothers, wives and husbands, mothers and fathers, women and men living together, working together as equals." Opinion polls showed that the majority of people in America were in favor of equal rights for all. Feminists were confident that democracy would not fail them.

NOW began organizing a Women's March on Washington, designed to make people aware of the importance of the ERA. It was specifically planned to get Congress to vote an extension, and is usually called the ERA Extension March. The date of the march, July 9, 1978, was the anniversary of the death of suffragist Alice Paul, one of the early fighters for women's rights. The march itself would be a copy of another Washington march, held more than fifty years ago, when women fought for the right to vote. As did those early suffragists, marchers planned to wear white and to carry banners of purple, gold, and white. They would even walk along the same route, stopping at the place where the suffragists had been physically attacked and beaten by men who opposed allowing women to vote.

The day of the march was hot and humid. The organizers were hoping for a crowd of twenty to thirty thousand supporters to join them, but worried that the weather would keep them away. As eleven o'clock approached, busloads and planeloads of people began arriving from all over the country. Gloria, one of the women leading the march towards the Capitol, was as excited as everyone else when she heard the crowd's size estimated at thirty thousand people, making this march the largest feminist gathering ever. As she stepped up to the speaker's podium a few hours later, she looked out at a sea of men and women, dressed in white, holding aloft their signs and banners. Gloria felt proud to have shared in this special event, and to be a part of such a noble and worthwhile cause. She knew that her friend, Stan Pottinger, a continued supporter of equal rights for women, was in the crowd. With him were his children, Paul and Katie, who had also been eager to be with her this day. Paul carried a sign that read "Equal Rights for All." Little Katie had a smaller sign suspended from a string around her neck stating "Kids for ERA."

When the rally was over, many people felt it had been a grand success. The next day, newspapers estimated the crowd to be one hundred thousand, many more than the organizers had dared to hope for. This outpouring of support may have influenced lawmakers; the U.S. House of Representatives approved a thirty-nine-month extension of the ERA by a vote of 233 to 189. In October, the Senate followed the lead of the House and voted to give the Equal Rights Amendment more time in which to be ratified. The new deadline for ratification was June 30, 1982. There was a great deal of work still to be done, but now there were several more years in which to do it.

Although Gloria had taken time off from her editorial position at *Ms.* for her Woodrow Wilson Fellowship work, she had contributed several articles during the year. Five days a week she had lived in Washington, D.C., doing research at the Library of Congress and the old red-brick Smithsonian Institution building on the Mall. On weekends, she flew up to New York to keep up-to-date with the magazine. She had also found time for ERA fundraising activities and speeches.

One speech in particular had been a very special one for Gloria to give—a commencement address delivered at Antioch School of Law in Washington, D.C. One of the members of the graduating class of 1978 was Susanne Patch, Gloria's sister. Sue had married early in the 1950s, at the age of thirty, after pursuing a career as a gemologist, an expert on precious stones. She had six children, and when they were grown, she had returned to school for a law degree. Gloria was very proud of Sue and all that she had accomplished. And Sue, too, felt pride that her little sister, the baby she herself had named so long ago in Clark Lake, was the honored co-speaker at her graduation.

At the end of her year of research, Gloria shared in publishing *The Decade of Women*, a history of women in the 1970s. The book was put together by Harriet Lyons and Susanne Levine, with an introduction written by Gloria. Full of photographs and information on the progress, achievements, setbacks, and disappointments of women over the previous ten years, the book won the Women in Communications Clarion Award for 1980. She also wrote the introduction for a book on the National Women's Conference in Houston.

Then, in 1981, the busy routine that filled Gloria's days was shattered. Ruth Steinem, Gloria's mother, died. Ruth had not been in the best of health and had spent these last few years in a nursing home near Sue's house. Her death, occurring just before her eighty-second birthday, was painful for both Gloria and Sue. There were so many good memories—happy times, when they had laughed together at family jokes, gone on vacations, shopped, and exchanged gifts. Even the difficult years of Gloria's childhood seemed far away now, and somehow, not quite so grim. Gloria remembered how, when she was older, her mother had managed to come with her on two speaking assignments, and how she had played softball with Sue's boys, her grandsons, when she was seventy-five years old.

After the funeral, while going through her mother's possessions, Gloria was moved when she found a small manuscript written by Ruth. It was a journal she had kept of a trip abroad, called "Grandma Goes to Europe." Ruth had never shown this journal to anyone, but, finding it, Gloria realized that her mother had continued to think of herself as a writer.

A few years after Ruth Steinem's death Gloria would write: "I miss her; but no more in death than I did in life. Dying seems less sad than having lived too little. But at least we're now asking questions about all the Ruths and all our family mysteries."

It was very clear to Gloria that the women's movement had changed women's lives, and perhaps could have changed her mother's life had it come twenty years sooner. Knowing this only strengthened her commitment to getting the ERA passed. It was running into resistance from many people, men and women.

Those against the ERA based their opposition on many grounds. Some worried about what would happen to families if women all returned to work; many felt that men would no longer be required to support their families. Others were concerned that equal rights meant women would have to be in the army with men, or would mean that women and men could not have separate bathrooms. The reassurances of many feminists familiar with the law, who knew these worries were without basis, did not succeed in convincing a majority of the states' representatives.

Even with Gloria's commitment and the continued work of many people, the ERA lost ground. No
amount of marches and speeches and explanations
seemed able to stem the tide of the reaction against the
Equal Rights Amendment. With a new president, Ron-
ald Reagan, against the ERA as well, its chances of
passage died. To the women who had worked so hard
for this bill, it had been a simple matter of fairness. It
was difficult for them to believe that it would not be
passed. They vowed to reintroduce it in the near future.

Despite these setbacks—indeed, because of them—
June 4, 1982, was a special day not just for Gloria but
for all the *Ms.* staff. It marked the tenth anniversary of
the founding of *Ms.* magazine. To celebrate, 1,200 people gathered for a party in New York City.

Ms. tried to make the event as large and festive as
possible. One reason for the gala party was to show that
even though the ERA had suffered a setback, feminist
goals were still supported by a majority in America.
After a disappointment, the *Ms.* staff felt that women,
especially, needed a chance to celebrate.

At the *Ms.* party, the guests tried hard to enjoy the
food and drinks, the music, and the dancing. Gloria
urged the guests to dance, reminding them of the words
of a famous revolutionary woman of the early 1900s,
Emma Goldman, who had once jokingly said, "If
there's no dancing, it's not my revolution." But beneath
the pleasant chatter of a party was a sense of anger and
disappointment. The new deadline for ERA, June 30,

1982, clearly would not be met. "I'm heartbroken," said Elizabeth Joel (owner of her own record company and at that time, married to singer Billy Joel). "I needed to be with a group that would understand."

Other women were optimistic. Pat Carbine, publisher of *Ms.*, felt it was "important to acknowledge. . . that we are in a very long process for full equality, and it is important to celebrate our victories." And Gloria, standing next to Pat and smiling for the press photographers, admitted, "I am angry but not disheartened." She reminded everyone of how much the women's rights movement had accomplished. "There is not a city or town without a women's center or a battered-wives hot line," she said.

At the end of the evening, amidst balloons and flowers and music, a giant two-tiered birthday cake was wheeled out onto the floor. Gloria and Pat cut the cake while Bella Abzug led the crowd in singing "Happy Birthday to *Ms.*"

Chapter/Ten

Outrageous Acts

In 1983 Gloria's book came out. It was a collection of her writings called *Outrageous Acts and Everyday Rebellions*. She had spent years planning, had seen years of postponement and delay, but finally was able to choose which articles to include and edit them. Even though many of the essays included had already been printed in magazines, there had still been a great deal of work. Each piece had to be updated, checked over, and given a place in the order of the book.

Gloria had never been very good at those kinds of details. Her friend, Letty Cottin Pogrebin, once said lovingly about Gloria, "She can't organize her life. She can't keep track of her papers or find her income tax returns." However, Letty went on to explain, "all her other competencies [superior abilities] are so overwhelming" that this weakness is what makes Gloria so endearing to her.

Letty had gone through boxes of Gloria's past writing and had shown a sampling to the publisher. The publisher's interest finally forced her reluctant friend to work on the book. Even before that, Joanne Edgar, another editor at *Ms.*, had spent years encouraging Gloria to collect her work in a book.

Struggling with the details had been difficult, but in the end Gloria felt it had been worth the effort. The book was an immediate success, and her publisher arranged speaking tours for her to publicize it. She appeared on many radio and television shows, telling audiences about the women's movement, answering questions about her life and work, and explaining what the title of her new book meant.

Interviewers always asked, "Exactly what is an 'outrageous act'?" Gloria would explain that, whenever she spoke, she would encourage women to change their lives by starting with small things. Do "at least one outrageous thing in the cause of simple justice during the next twenty-four hours" she would urge them. That act can be as small as saying, "Pick it up yourself," to a member of the family or as large as calling a strike at work to protest unfairness. Gloria would promise her audiences that if they did that, "the world one day later won't be quite the same." That was the kind of rebellion Gloria had in mind when she had named her book.

Many of the essays Gloria had written had been a kind of rebellion, too. Certainly some of them were considered outrageous when they appeared originally.

The pieces, "If Men Could Menstruate" and "In Praise of Women's Bodies," were the sort of writing that shocked many people. Even her political profiles, or her essays on famous women like the actress Marilyn Monroe or Patricia (Pat) Nixon, the wife of President Richard Nixon, had been different from ordinary interviews.

But for Gloria personally, the most revolutionary of all her essays was the one she had written especially for this book, titled "Ruth's Song (Because She Could Not Sing It)." This piece revealed for the first time Gloria's difficult childhood and the once-hidden details of her mother's illness. As a child and a young adult, Gloria had been ashamed of that part of her life. In this essay, she wondered why it had taken her so many years to understand that the forces that shaped her mother's life were "patterns women share," and admitted sadly that "the world still missed a unique person named Ruth."

That single article caused much discussion and inspired reporters and interviewers to ask many questions. Gloria answered these questions on a sensitive topic as honestly as she could. She discovered that many people had gone through similar childhoods with mothers who had suffered in the same way. These people confessed to Gloria that they, too, had kept their family secret, telling no one, and never questioning, until they read her book, why their mothers had not been helped.

Sharing and discussing these childhood memories was one of the positive results of publishing *Outrageous*

Acts and Everyday Rebellions. Another was that, while promoting the book, she had the chance to travel not only in America, but to England, and again to Japan. In that country she was introduced to the growing awareness of Asian women's social inequality.

Japanese women had no security for their jobs. Discrimination based on sex was legal in Japan; if an employer did not wish to have a woman in a particular job, there was no law to say that he had to give a woman a chance at that job. The women were just learning to find ways to protest such treatment.

Japanese women and their problems formed a sharp contrast to women in other less developed countries where Gloria had previously traveled. A trip to Egypt several years before had had an especially strong impact on her. Here, she had been accompanied by her friend Laila Abou Saif, who was an Egyptian and a leading feminist in her native country.

In Egypt, as in many Muslim lands, most women were still subject to the will of their fathers, even in choosing a marriage partner. Once married, they had to obey their husbands. Egyptian women worked very hard in their homes, and many were still completely veiled when they went outside their homes to shop or visit relatives. Gloria's heart had gone out to these women, still at the very beginning of the struggle for equality. She knew there were millions of women all over the world living like those she met in Egypt.

Other aspects of her publicity tour were less serious.

When she was featured on "20/20," one of the most popular interview shows on television, hosted by pioneer woman newscaster Barbara Walters, Gloria showed another side of herself to TV audiences. At Barbara's request, she did a tap dance to a popular old tune, "For Me and My Gal," sung by Barbara. (The two women would repeat that performance a few years later at Carnegie Hall, in a show to raise money for the New York Pops Orchestra.)

That was not the only time Gloria succeeded in surprising people by doing the unexpected. She was indeed a feminist who cared deeply about equal rights for all, and she was often angry about injustices done to women, but that didn't mean she couldn't laugh, too. The best lesson Gloria had learned from her friend Flo Kennedy, one of the women with whom she had toured America and shared a speaker's podium, was that "a revolution without humor was as hopeless as one without music." Gloria never forgot that, and her natural sense of humor usually doesn't stay hidden for long.

Perhaps it was that love of fun that led her, later in 1983, to agree to pose relaxing in a bubble bath for a woman photographer. The photo appeared in *People* magazine and showed Gloria with her hair casually pinned up behind her head, and her body hidden beneath heaps of foaming soap bubbles. Immediately after the issue came out, there were reactions to the photo. Most people laughed about it, but others expressed shock or dismay and used it to criticize Gloria. Gloria soon realized that it had been a mistake to allow the photo to be taken.

For many people, publicity is often difficult to deal with, especially when it seems unfair or misleading. Although being seen by thousands of people in a bubble bath was not so bad, Gloria could remember other times which were awful. Many times she had been personally attacked by people opposed to the causes she supported. One of the worst incidents had been in 1972. *Esquire* magazine published an article that accused her of using her men friends to help her succeed in publishing. Gloria had been so embarrassed by the conclusions drawn by the article's author that she said she "wanted to crawl into a hole" to hide. She had also been angry, and even thought about suing the author and *Esquire.* But later, she came to believe that accusations like those were a standard way of explaining women's success. Discussing the way that many people viewed women's relationships to men in the workplace, she said bitterly, "They either tell you that you use men for social climbing, or that you're a lesbian." Once she understood that such attacks were a way to lessen the value of her ideas by making her success appear to be unearned, their sting faded.

The year 1984 arrived. It was hard to believe that a decade had passed since Gloria's fortieth birthday. In just a couple of months, she would celebrate her fiftieth year. Her friends kept telling her they could not believe it—Gloria looked young, attractive, and vigorous to them. She had enough plans to fill a lifetime and more.

Gloria herself found it hard to believe that she was nearing fifty. Inside, she still carried the little girl who had once lived in Toledo, and had studied and dreamed and struggled for a better life—a life that was now hers.

"We have become the men we wanted to marry," she said several years before in a speech at Yale University. In another speech, this one in Hartford, Connecticut, she pointed out: "The last twelve to fifteen years have created changes in our dreams." By this she meant that many women who once dreamed of merely marrying successful men now wanted to be successful themselves.

Gloria was one of those successful women. And after many years of saying she was not yet ready to marry, she finally realized that she was happy without marrying. Once quoted as saying, "I will not get married until the Equal Rights Amendment is passed," she now says that is not the only reason, although it is a major one. "We need laws and values that make marriage a real partnership," she says, and hopes that young women will be able to choose what is best for themselves today and in the future.

Not only does the choice not to marry represent a change; ideas about marriage have also changed. That fact is reflected in our language, says Gloria. "We now have words like 'sexual harassment,' 'displaced home-maker,' and 'battered woman'. . .Ten years ago it was just called life."

These are some of the things Gloria tells her audiences when she is introduced to her usual standing-room-only crowd. Once frightened of public speaking, she now faces audiences with less nervousness. In an even, conversational tone she explains things exactly the way she sees them and leaves her listeners nodding their heads in agreement and clapping enthusiastically.

Combining optimism and activism, Gloria smilingly tells audiences: "Together we have come through the first decade of the second wave of feminism in this country." The "first wave" was the time women fought for the right to vote, and Gloria is quick to recall that "it took 100 to 150 years to take that step forward." Knowing this, women should not be discouraged, says Gloria. "We probably have another 90 to 140 years to go." Nevertheless, there have been many changes.

Gloria does not mind being seen as a radical, a label that many people have given her. "Feminists are always thought of as radical," she says. "The truth is we're sweetly reasonable. It's the system that is radically wrong." Gloria smiles when she says that, knowing it will often be met with disbelief, even though she herself is convinced that the statement is true.

Fairness is an important idea for Gloria. She feels it is a concept that all young people—boys as well as girls—can easily understand, and that is the message she tries to deliver. In part she has succeeded. She is called the "foremost spokesperson" for the feminist movement, and a woman who has "shaped our times."

When Gloria's fiftieth birthday celebration was
planned, it was meant to be a celebration of the
women's movement, too. Nevertheless, it was Gloria's
friends, admirers, and co-workers who planned and
organized it, chief among them her friends Letty Cottin Pogrebin, Marlo Thomas, and Pat Carbine. The
"honorary chairs" for the event were four famous wom-
en: Betty Ford, an activist for women's rights and the
wife of past president Gerald Ford; Billie Jean King,
champion of women's tennis; Sally Ride, the first
American woman astronaut to take a journey into
space; and Alice Walker, prize-winning writer and a
close friend. Others at this celebration were men and
women from all walks of life who had one thing in
common: an admiration for feminist leader Gloria
Steinem.

Stan Pottinger, her special friend, escorted her into
the Grand Ballroom at the Waldorf Astoria Hotel in
New York City, where her birthday party took place.
She was dressed in an elegant, long evening gown. Her
blonde-streaked, shoulder-length hair shone, and a
warm, glowing smile lit up her face. Even though she
had known all along that the party was being planned,
and had followed its progress, she still gasped with
delight at the sight of the room, so beautifully decorated in pink and white, and the crowds of people who
had come to pay her tribute.

Moved by the speeches and the feelings of love and
friendship, and overwhelmed by the birthday greetings

which poured in from every side, the evening blended into one whirl of pleasant emotion and excitement for her. A silver-colored "Birthday Book" was printed and given to every guest. It contained many birthday greetings to Gloria. Among the greetings was one which read, "You helped me to achieve the me I could be. Love from one sister to another." It was a moving tribute to Gloria from a friend, and brought to mind another compliment Gloria had received. At a local tenth-anniversary celebration of *Ms.* magazine held in Detroit, a small, gray-haired woman with "hardworking hands" had come up to tell Gloria, "I just want you to know that you are the inside of me."

"All reward came together in one moment," Gloria had written about that incident in her book. The compliment meant so much because it represented the results that she hoped to achieve. She wanted to reach out not just to the famous people, but to ordinary working women, to help change their lives and their dreams, just as Gloria had changed her own.

Already past her fiftieth birthday now, Gloria Steinem continues working for her goal of a fair world where there will be complete equality for women and men of all races, no matter how they choose to live. "The point is not the choice we make," she stresses, "the point is the power to make a choice."

Gloria would like women to be "taken seriously." "If I could wave a wand and produce a magical result," she says, "I would want women's self-respect to grow so we could speak for ourselves; talk for ourselves." Her own "four great goals" remain very much the same as they have been for the past ten years: reproductive freedom for women; honoring and giving greater value to work traditionally done by women, including putting a specific monetary value on childrearing and other jobs in the home; making families more democratic by convincing couples to share childrearing; and taking the politics out of culture so that women's lives and problems are taken as seriously as those of men. (This theme would be taken up in a 1986 book she wrote about Marilyn Monroe, an actress who was often not taken seriously as an acting professional.)

To help achieve her goals for women, Gloria Steinem continues as a feminist speaker, organizer, and writer. Her life has been and continues to be a model of independence, spirit, and idealism. For many young women, she is an example of the new and vital role of women of all ages in American society.

Afterword

A note from Gloria Steinem

It's very odd to read about one's life. If each of you imagines all the change and happenstance of your own life in a book like this, you'll see what I mean.

But there are unexpected rewards, especially when you have two authors who are as thorough and hardworking as Emily Taitz and Sondra Henry.

For one thing, Emily and Sondra have helped me to see a longer view of my life: to look at the shape of the forest, instead of getting caught up only in the individual reality of its day-to-day trees. I'm going to try to remember this lesson as I think about the future. Daily decisions that seem small are still brush strokes in a larger painting. That's a guide to the good use of time. And time is all there is.

For another thing, the painstaking research of these authors has restored some life experiences that had gotten obscured for me. For instance, they researched facts about my suffragist grandmother, who died when I was too young to really know her. I will treasure the lessons she bequeathed as an activist foremother of us all, as well as someone who influenced my family and therefore me. Emily and Sondra even went to my college to unearth reports from my fellowship years in India that I myself had forgotten writing. I'm grateful for these and other gifts that have renewed or expanded a view of the past.

But they also have asked me to note some future plans that will continue the story you just read.

For myself, I hope:

- to continue my commitment to *Ms.* magazine, still the only national magazine for women that is actually controlled by women.
- to spend more time doing what matters most to me: writing. I have resolved this so often that I'm a little ashamed to say it one more time, but perhaps recording it here will strengthen my resolve. For instance, I am planning a book about women in powerful families (and how this power is more often passed *through* them than *to* them), plus a book about self-esteem (the loss of which is one of the deepest punishments for any group or individual), plus a long overdue book on feminist theory in its simplest and most universal form. I would also like to write scripts for

movies, which are such an influence on all our lives and dreams. In fact, I am now working on one that is based on some of the more personal essays in *Outrageous Acts and Everyday Rebellions.* I would like to write the stories of very old women in this society, who are often the most courageous of us all; I want to write down personal stories that strangers tell me, simply because I am accidentally a recognizable part of a change that means a great deal to millions of women's and men's and children's lives; I would like to write more humor, for laughter makes us see ironies that tears obscure; I would like to write about feminist organizing by women in Third World countries, so that international feminist learning becomes more of a two-way street....Well, as you can see, I have much to do. Only time will tell if I can do it.

We also can't live by work alone. I am looking forward to much more dancing in my life, to saving money and planning better for the future, to making my apartment a more organized and cheerful place to come home to, and to seeing much more of the friends who are support, learning, and love to me.

For you who read this, and for all the great social justice movements that free our talents and give us life, I hope:

- that we will never allow ourselves to be divided. Racial caste systems are intertwined with and dependent on sex discrimination—and vice versa. These two deepest of all revolutions must be fought together, or both will fail. And if we divide ourselves by class or sexual preference, we only reduce our own forces and the strength of our own moral position.
- that we understand the long view, and build change into the full length of our lives. Thousands of years of sexual and racial bias, of the lie that some people are intrinsically "worth more" than others, may be overcome in centuries. They cannot be overcome in decades.

But, if we work to free human talents, we are rewarded by discovering our own.

You who are reading this book will go even farther than the rest of us. You are the future. Emily and Sondra have written about one person's path. The hope we share is that this helps you to discover your own.

—*Gloria Steinem*

Appendix

A Brief History of the Women's Rights Movement

The women's rights movement in the United States had its beginnings in 1840, when two women, Elizabeth Cady Stanton and Lucretia Mott, went to the World Anti-Slavery Convention in London, England. Lucretia Mott was one of eight women delegates who were denied seats because of their sex. Elizabeth Cady Stanton was the wife of a delegate. Both were indignant at the way women were being treated at the convention. When they met, they decided that after returning to the United States they would start an organization to advance the rights of women.

It took eight years before the first Women's Rights Convention was held in Seneca Falls, New York. Elizabeth Cady Stanton and Lucretia Mott put a notice in a local newspaper inviting people to come on July 19 and 20, 1848. Three hundred people attended that first meeting.

The most shocking proposition to come out of this convention was: "It is the duty of the women of this country to secure to themselves their sacred right to the elective franchise." This resolution meant that women were asking for the right to vote. It was included in the Declaration of Sentiments, along with a list of the women's complaints and twelve demands for rights.

Susan B. Anthony, a teacher who had long been involved in anti-slavery meetings and in the Temperance Movement (an organization that worked to stop the use of alcohol), joined the new women's movement early in the 1850s. In 1852 Elizabeth Cady Stanton asked her to help draft a petition for "full and total" property rights for women in New York. The three things they asked for in this petition were that:

1. Women should control their own earnings.
2. Women should be allowed to vote in all elections.
3. Women should have guardianship of their children if they were divorced.

Control by women of their own money and property was not a new issue. Ernestine Rose, a Polish-Jewish immigrant to America, had worked for twelve years, from 1836 to 1848, for the final passage of the New York State Married Woman's Property Act. This gave women, rather than their husbands, the right to control property that they owned before they got married or inherited after their marriage.

Once this became law, Susan B. Anthony and Elizabeth Cady Stanton began to campaign for the right of women to control any wages that they earned. Until that time, they had to turn their salaries over to their fathers or husbands. The passage of this bill also took twelve years, and did not become law until 1860.

While the women were struggling for their rights, the nation had become involved in the Civil War and the issue of slavery. In 1865 when the war ended, many women fought for the right of former slaves to become citizens and vote. They hoped that women might also gain suffrage at this time. Yet when the Fifteenth Amendment was ratified in 1870, it stated that no citizens should be denied the right to vote because of "race, color, or previous condition of servitude." It did not include women.

In 1869 two important women's organizations were formed—The National Women's Suffrage Association, and the American Women's Suffrage Association. The object of the National Association was to achieve a federal amendment guaranteeing suffrage, and of the American, to gain suffrage state by state.

In 1875 Susan B. Anthony drew up the proposed constitutional amendment: "The right of citizens of the United States to vote shall not be denied or abridged by the United States or by any state on account of sex." This amendment was first brought up in Congress in 1878 and took forty-five years, until 1920, to become law.

In 1890 the two women's organizations joined together to become the National American Woman Suffrage Association (NAWSA). Their goal was "to secure protection, in their right to vote, to the women citizens of the United States, by appropriate national and state legislation."

In 1902 Elizabeth Cady Stanton, one of the founders of the women's movement, died. Just four years later, Susan B. Anthony also died, leaving the women's rights movement without a strong leader.

It was not until after 1910 that the issue of women's rights was brought back to life by Alice Paul, a social worker and a militant feminist. While studying social work in England, she was impressed by the daring deeds of the English women who were fighting for their rights, especially Emmeline Pankhurst and her daughters. When Alice Paul returned from England, she was determined to reactivate the American women's rights movement by using some of the same tactics that the Pankhursts had. She led American women into another wave of feminism with demonstrations, picketing, hunger strikes, and political activism.

Alice Paul brought the issue of women's suffrage to the attention of the public again. In 1913 she led a march of thousands of women down Pennsylvania Avenue in Washington, D.C., braving insults and jeers from spectators. Because of her activism, she was expelled from NAWSA when Carrie Chapman Catt returned as president in 1915.

At this time, many women thought that force should not be used to get the vote and did not even want woman's suffrage to become an issue of party politics. They thought they could win the vote in a peaceful manner. Alice Paul did not agree with that approach. She organized the National Woman's Party with one issue in mind: the vote for women.

By 1916 women had obtained full, equal suffrage in eleven states and the territory of Alaska, and partial suffrage in some other states. Both major U.S. political parties had adopted a women's suffrage plank.

On May 21, 1919, after many defeats, the House of Representatives of the sixty-sixth Congress passed the Nineteenth Amendment by a vote of 304 to 90. The Senate followed on June 4, passing it 66 to 30. However, it took until August 18, 1920, for the thirty-sixth state, Tennessee, to ratify it. At last, on August 26, 1930, the Nineteenth Amendment to the Constitution gave women the right to vote. Seventy-two years had passed since that first Women's Rights Convention at Seneca Falls.

After women got the vote, the women's rights movement seemed to fade from the American scene. During the civil rights movement in the 1960s, women began to realize once again that they were not considered equal to men. At that time women held one-third of all the jobs in the United States. Some began to feel that women should first campaign for their own rights before they fought for the rights of others.

In 1963 *The Feminine Mystique,* by Betty Friedan, was published. This important book told about many women who wanted more in their lives than just marriage and family. It pointed out that housewives often felt bored and useless. The ideas in Betty Friedan's book, along with the interest in women's rights—equality in jobs, pay, education, and family life—created the newest wave of feminism. This new movement spurred many changes in American life and law, such as the Civil Rights Act of 1964. Included in this bill was Title VII, which outlawed discrimination, or unfair treatment, on the basis of race, color, religion, national origin, or sex.

In 1966 Friedan founded the National Organization for Women (NOW). Its purpose was to win an equal place for women in American society. The Equal Rights Amendment (ERA) to the Constitution, which would further that goal, was first introduced in Congress in 1923 through the work of the National Woman's Party. The amendment states: "Equality of rights under the law shall not be denied or abridged by the United States or any state on account of sex." Congress did pass the ERA in 1972, but it did not win the approval of the necessary three-fourths (thirty-eight) of the state legislatures. Thirty-five states, three short of the needed number, ratified the ERA by the 1982 deadline for its approval. Because it did not pass, it must be introduced in Congress again and go through the same ratification process if it is to become law.

Bibliography

Achbar, Francine. "Steinem Calls for 'Humanizing of White Male Ruling Class'." *Boston Sunday Herald Traveler* (October 3, 1971).

Barthel, Joan. "The Glorious Triumph of Gloria Steinem." *Cosmopolitan* (March, 1984), 217-219.

Bumiller, Elizabeth. "Gloria Steinem: Two Decades of Feminism and the Fire Burns as Bright." *Washington Post* (October 12, 1983).

"David Frost Show." Tape of 1972 TV show. Gloria Steinem, host.

Dullea, Georgia. "Birthday Celebration: Gloria Steinem at 50." *New York Times* (May 24, 1984).

Edmiston, Susan. "How To Say What You Mean and Get What You Want." *Redbook* (March, 1976), 94.

Gilbert, Lynn. *Particular Passions*. New York: Clarkson N. Potter, 1981.

"A Girl—Signed Herself." *Glamour* (February, 1964), 106-109.

"Gloria Steinem Honored by UN Organization." *Christian Science Monitor* (December 11, 1975).

Gold, Doris. Interview with authors. New York, November 15, 1985.

"Influence: Ten Most Influential Women in America." *Harper's Bazaar* (September, 1983), 202.

Kennedy, Flo. *Color Me Flo: My Hard Life and Good Times.* New Jersey: Prentice-Hall, 1976.

Kitman, Marvin. "A Most Revealing 'Bunny'." *Newsday* (February 25, 1985).

Klemesrud, Judy. "A Reporter's Notebook: History Lesson For Feminists." *New York Times* (July 11, 1983).

Kramer, Sylvia. Telephone interview with authors. New York, May 28, 1985.

Levitt, Leonard. "She: The Awesome Power of Gloria Steinem." *Esquire* (October, 1971), 87.

Little, Gayle. "Gloria Steinem Bares Sex Myths." *Toledo Times* (October 17, 1970).

Mercer, M. "*McCall's* Woman of the Year." *McCall's* (January, 1972), 67-69.

Ms. Numerous articles from 1972 to 1985.

New York Times. Numerous articles from January 1964 to January 1986.

Patch, Susanne Steinem. Telephone interview with authors. Washington, D.C., November 20, 1985.

Pogrebin, Letty Cottin. Telephone interview with authors. New York, December 10, 1985.

Rapaport, Florence. Interview with authors. Great Neck, N.Y., June 21, 1985.

Reef, Betty. "Pretty Girl Genius Helps Edit *Help! For*

Tired Minds." The Oklahoman (November 13, 1960).

"Reporters: Thinking Man's Shrimpton." *Time* (January 3, 1969), 38.

Sawyer, Susan G. "Sisterhood is Powerful." *Daily News Magazine* (August 18, 1985), 13.

Sheehy, Gail. "Hers." *New York Times* (January 31, 1980).

"Speaking With Steinem—Always Provocative Feminist Hosts a Probing TV Interview Show." *Christian Science Monitor* (March 16, 1984).

Steinem, Gloria. Interviews with authors. New York, July 12, 1985; October 24, 1985; January 22, 1986; December 18, 1986.

———. "After Black Power, Women's Liberation." *New York* (April 7, 1969), 8-9.

———. "A Bunny's Tale: *Show's* First Exposé for Intelligent People." *Show* (May and June, 1963).

———. "College and What I Learned There." *Glamour* (August, 1964), 148.

———. India series of articles. *The Sophian* (Smith College newspaper) (October 24, 1954; November 7, 1957; November 12, 1957; November 21, 1957; December 12, 1957; October 14, 1958.)

———. "Looking Around with Gloria Steinem: *What* Culture." *Look* (November 26, 1968), 18.

———. "The Moral Disarmament of Betty Co-ed." *Esquire* (September, 1962), 97.

———. *Ms.* Numerous articles from 1972 to 1985.

———. *Outrageous Acts and Everyday Rebellions.* New York: Holt, Rinehart & Winston, 1983.

———. "The Politics of Women." Commencement Address, May 30, 1971. *Smith Alumnae Quarterly* (August, 1971), 13-17.

———. "What *Playboy* Doesn't Know About Women Could Fill a Book." (Interview with Hugh Hefner, publisher of *Playboy* magazine.) *McCall's* (October, 1970), 76-77.

Stephen, Beverly. "I'm Your Bunny, Gloria." *Daily News* (February 24, 1985).

Toledo *Blade.* Articles from September 12, 1958; November 14, 1965; October 17, 1970; May 10, 1972; March 13, 1979.

Wadler, Joyce. "The Feminist at Fifty: A Glittery Birthday Bash for Gloria Steinem." *Washington Post* (May 24, 1984).

Index